# Money
# the Internet

JONQUIL LOWE

**WHICH?**
**BOOKS**

CONSUMERS' ASSOCIATION

Which? Books are commissioned by

Consumers' Association and published by
Which? Ltd, 2 Marylebone Road, London NW1 4DF
Email address: books@which.net

Distributed by The Penguin Group:

Penguin Books Ltd, 80 Strand, London WC2R 0RL

First edition September 2001
Bound in new cover 2004

British Library Cataloguing in Publication Data

A catalogue record for this book is available from the British Library

ISBN 0 85202 962 4

For a full list of Which? books, please call 0800 252100, access our
website at www.which.net, or write to Which? Books, Freepost, PO
Box 44, Hertford SG14 1SH

Editorial and production: Joanna Bregosz, Nithya Rae

Original cover concept by Sarah Harmer

Cover photograph by Antonio M. Rosario/getty images

Typeset by Saxon Graphics Ltd, Derby

Printed and bound in Great Britain by Clays Ltd, St Ives plc

# Contents

* An asterisk next to the name of an organisation in the text indicates that the web site or address can be found in these sections

# Introduction

By May 2001, two out of every five UK homes (some 10 million in all) were connected to the Internet, according to the telecommunications regulator, Oftel. In the space of just a year, the number of connected homes had risen by 4 million. However, despite this huge and growing interest in the online world, the number of people using the Internet to manage their personal finances remains low.

A survey for the Financial Services Authority (FSA),* which regulates many financial products and services in the UK, found that about one in every 11 adults banks online, one in 20 surfs the Net for financial information, one in 50 carries out share-dealing online, and three in 100 shop around for financial products online. Even these figures might overestimate the true position – a survey by online analyst Gomez found that one person in every ten who sign up for Internet banking stops using his or her online account within six months.

Look far enough into the future and it is easy to imagine a world where we all deal with our money matters effortlessly from our home computer or television screen. It will seem unbelievable that we ever tramped from one high street branch to another searching for mortgage deals, stamped endless envelopes as we paid our bills, or rushed to catch the bank before the doors slammed shut at 4.30pm. As accounts are electronic, it makes sense to effect transfers from one account to another electronically too. And, in a market place crowded with thousands of financial products, what hope does one consumer have of finding the best product by laboriously gathering up brochures and soundbites from salespeople? It is far more sensible to consult a database that will help you narrow down your search to the handful of products with the features you want.

The biggest factor holding back our leap into this future is fear about security. Consumers worry about using their credit cards to shop online. They are uneasy about the safety of bank accounts and investments held in Internet accounts, and examples of high-profile errors where consumer data has been revealed on web sites have undermined confidence. Concerns about access have been prompted by bank and broking web sites crashing owing to an unanticipated volume of users. And, on top of this, Internet users have to cope with software problems on their own computers and faults on their phone lines. Hardly surprising, then, that consumers are wary of entrusting their financial fortunes to the fickle Web.

However, some of the fears are out of proportion to the real risks involved. Credit-card fraud is a problem mainly for retailers, who must generally foot the bill for any misuse. With the implementation of the Distance Selling Directive in the UK from October 2000, you are not liable for any loss caused by unauthorised use of your debit or credit cards to buy non-financial products over the Internet, and similar legislation to protect you when you buy financial products is due to be implemented in 2002. In the meantime, your maximum loss is in any case limited to £50. If your fears are still not allayed, other ways to shop on the Internet are available that limit your exposure even further. So really there is no reason not to take the plunge and buy, say, car or life insurance online.

The incidence of fraudsters intercepting secure Internet communications or hacking into web sites is very low indeed, so the chances of the contents of your bank savings or investment account being stolen are probably very low. But, of course, the consequences would be severe if this unlikely event were to happen. At present, most online providers leave you, the consumer, to bear any resulting loss in full. Notable exceptions are a growing number of online banking services that either limit your maximum loss to £50 or guarantee you will not be liable for any loss, provided you take sensible precautions to protect your security codes and personal identification numbers (PINs).

Note that not all banks protect you. Some, including Alliance & Leicester, Bank of Scotland, First-e, NatWest and Virgin may leave you exposed to unlimited losses if you are the victim of computer fraud. And online broking and investment fund services typically leave you similarly exposed. This is not dissimilar to the situation in the 1980s and early 1990s concerning 'phantom withdrawals' from cash machines. The banks claimed their cash machines were completely secure, and that any unauthorised withdrawals must have been the fault of the consumer who had either fraudulently made the withdrawals themselves or allowed their PIN to fall into the hands of another. The onus was on the consumer to prove his or her innocence – an often impossible task unless, for example, he or she fortuitously had a witness to provide an alibi for the time of a rogue withdrawal. This situation was eventually resolved in the consumers' favour by the introduction of a clause into the Banking Code limiting your loss on plastic cards of all types to a maximum of £50, provided you are not involved in a fraud and have not been careless with your security information. If financial providers want to encourage consumers to embrace the Internet, they need to be prepared to extend similar protection to online services.

Internet providers and regulators also need to be realistic in their expectations of consumers. To access an online service, you generally need an identification code, a password and sometimes other security information too. It is vital for the security of your accounts that you keep your details secret and safe from theft. The most sensible course is undoubtedly to memorise the information and not to write it down or store it anywhere. But how realistic is this, if you are going to have three or four – maybe more – online accounts, covering, say, a current account, savings account, share-dealing service, investment fund, insurance quotes, pension plan, and so on? Can you really memorise all these passwords? On top of this, it is good advice to change your passwords regularly – how will you cope with this too? Research for the FSA found that, in reality, 83 per cent of people using online banking or broking services write down their passwords and 50 per cent store them on their computers. Furthermore, 80 per cent of people never change their passwords.

There are currently three possible solutions to password overload. First, you could conduct all your online finances with a single provider, accessing all your accounts with a single password – the drawback, of course, is that it is unlikely that one provider will have the best product in every category.

The second option would be to use the same password with every provider. This is strongly frowned upon by providers and security experts but, from your point of view, it is no different from having all your accounts on a single web site that can be accessed with just one password.

Finally, you could use one of the new account aggregation services that draw together information about your accounts with different providers on to a single web site. The drawbacks here are that you may breach the security rules of the different providers and that, under current laws, aggregation services are unregulated, leaving you exposed if something goes wrong. Aggregation services have caught on in the USA and would seem a sensible way forward for UK consumers, but it is essential that the FSA is given powers to regulate these services.

Visit the web sites covered in this guide and you will see that all the main building blocks for managing your finances online are in place: you can bank, save and invest, buy insurance, take out a mortgage, and find credit cards and loans, all over the Net. You can even take out complicated products such as pensions, and the missing ingredient – financial advice – is gradually making its debut on the Web.

What the online financial world now lacks most is customers. Once the security issues have been properly addressed, the Internet deserves to flourish as a primary route for managing your finances, giving you unprecedented access to financial products, services and information, together with the tools you need to make informed and powerful choices.

*Note: The Internet is a big place and a fast-moving world. We make no pretence at providing comprehensive coverage. The web sites included in this guide are ones that we found useful, interesting or popular. But many more web sites are out there and, inevitably, some of the addresses we mention may alter or disappear. If you have favourite web sites that you would like to share with other readers in a future edition of this book, tell us about them by writing to books@which.net or* The Which? Guide to Money on the Internet, *Which? Books, 2 Marylebone Road, London NW1 4DF.*

# The story of 'e'

1

In 1983 the Nottingham Building Society and the Bank of Scotland together launched Homelink, the first home-banking system. Using a special adaptor or a home computer plus telephone and TV screen, customers linked into the bank's computer via Prestel (a system similar to Teletext but delivered via the phone rather than a TV aerial). They could then check their account, transfer money between their accounts and pay bills, even do a limited amount of shopping online or buy and sell shares.

Customers without a home computer who wished to use the home-banking service could pay £150 to buy the special equipment, or £41.10 a month to rent it, plus £2 a month subscription charge. Home computers at the time were likely to be one of the *Which?* best buys, such as an Acorn Electron (£200), BBC Model B (£400) or Sinclair ZX Spectrum 48K (£130). These were usually wired up to a TV, with programs probably stored on a portable cassette player. The computer itself had no hard memory, only 4 to 64 kilobytes of random access memory (RAM) that was wiped clean each time the computer was turned off.

The common opinion among users was that home banking was convenient but no substitute for traditional banking. Strangely, despite advanced technology, opinions remain much the same today. It is estimated that only about 9 per cent of UK adults use e-banking, compared with around 4 per cent who shop online. The majority of customers still prefer bricks-and-mortar banks. Experts predict that the most successful e-banks will be those that are simply offering the Internet as an additional way to access your account, rather than Internet-access-only banks, i.e. those that do not have bricks-and-mortar branches  (see Chapter 5).

# The Which? Guide to Money on the Internet

The limited availability of computers during the 1980s forced the pioneers of home banking to turn to equipment that was readily available in most homes – the television. What is surprising here is that, despite the growing popularity of home computers today (around two-fifths – 41 per cent – of UK adults have a PC at home), the future of mass-market e-finance seems still to rest with television. Experts predict that the take-up of e-services will see its next big leap only when digital TV is established in the majority of homes. Currently, around a quarter of UK households have digital TV.

Banking was an obvious service for providers of financial products and services to offer electronically. Computers began to be used internally by banks in the early 1960s, and automatic teller machines (ATMs) emerged in the 1970s. The following decade saw the introduction of electronic funds transfer at the point of sale (EFTPOS – a grand name for using plastic to pay for goods in shops), and in 1987 Barclay's Bank launched the first debit card. Given the cost of handling cash and running large branch networks, banks have had a strong incentive to convert customers to remote banking in all its forms. At the same time, there have also been potential advantages for consumers, in being able to do their banking without making repeated journeys to a branch.

There has been less of an incentive for suppliers of other goods and services to take the Internet route, because these suppliers are not usually so dependent on large branch-based networks (partly because transactions with them tend to be less frequent, whereas people interact with their bank on a day-to-day basis), and, unlike banks, they do not operate the money transmission system. (Think of the cost to banks of physically transporting cash around the country in armoured vans on a daily basis.) As the importance of the Internet has grown, many providers of financial products and services have recognised the need to have a corporate presence on the Web, and in the last few years the growth of web sites selling financial products and services has mushroomed.

At the forefront of this growth have been share-dealing services. Most private stockbroking has traditionally been handled at a distance by phone, and so it was a small step for brokers to begin accepting orders by Internet as well. A more dramatic breakthrough has been the emergence of web sites that give direct access to the stock market.

Among the slowest to embrace the Web have been insurance companies. A survey by the Association of British Insurers (ABI) in 2000 found that over three-quarters (78 per cent) of those members who responded had a web site, but only two-fifths of these sites were being used as a way of producing direct sales. The two-thirds of the association's members who did not reply to the survey possibly had even less interest in selling via the Internet.

However, some insurance intermediaries have embraced the Web, and with great success. A National Opinion Poll (NOP) survey in March 2001 found that car insurance is the financial product that Internet users are most likely to buy online. Over a quarter (27 per cent) of Internet users had searched for car insurance quotes, and of these 21 per cent went on to buy. Experts say car insurance is an ideal Internet product: it is relatively low value, therefore consumers are less anxious about the security aspect, and it is a repeat purchase, so consumers are able to build up familiarity and confidence.

The next most popular financial product with online users is mortgages. NOP found that 17 per cent of users had sought out online information about home loans, but only 1 in 20 (5 per cent) went on to buy over the Web.

Use of the Internet for making large investments is even lower. It seems that when it comes to major financial transactions – particularly those that are made infrequently, such as taking out a mortgage or investing a lump sum – most people prefer to deal face-to-face. This has also been the story with financial advice, which so far has failed to take off as an e-service.

For consumers happy to take the e-plunge, there are a growing number of financial supermarkets usually offering products at discounted prices. Some specialise in investment funds – mainly unit trusts – but increasingly these sites are expanding to include a wide range of other products, with the aim of becoming one-stop financial shops.

A survey for the Financial Services Consumer Panel found that overall, only 2 per cent of financial products are currently purchased via the Internet or digital TV. This compares with 36 per cent buying at a branch or office of the provider or an adviser, and 25 per cent through a salesperson visiting the customer's home (see the chart below).

## How financial products are taken out

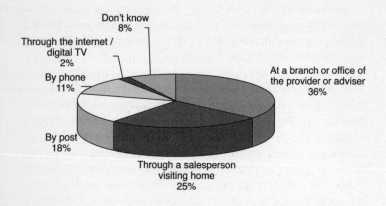

*Source: BMRB survey for Financial Services Consumer Panel, 2000.*

The progress of e-finance is being held back partly by the legal framework. In particular, most financial agreements require a signature before they are valid. So you can find the product you want online, check out its terms and conditions and fill in an application form. However, at the last hurdle you will probably discover you need to print off the form, so that you can sign it and then return it to the financial firm via traditional post. In May 2000 the Electronic Communications Act was passed. This allows for digital signatures (a code incorporated into a document that identifies you in the same way as a written signature) to be accepted, and so clears the way for completing the whole transaction online. Unfortunately, the section of the Act dealing with digital signatures is being brought into force by means of regulations, and, at the time of writing, the various government departments concerned had still not finalised these.

Further legal inconvenience stems from money-laundering regulations. To combat the legitimising of money from illegal activities, such as drug dealing, financial providers are required to check the identity of people who open accounts or make investments. Typically, a bank or building society will need to see a passport, driving licence or similar document to establish your identity, and a recent household bill, say, to verify your address, which makes it impossible to deal completely online. Providers can sometimes avoid this process by requiring that you open an account or investment with a cheque drawn on, or an electronic transfer from, another account that has the same name as the one you will be using to hold the investment. In this way the provider can rely on the identity checks already made by the bank or building society of the original account.

However, the biggest brake on e-finance is consumer doubt, particularly with regard to security. The safety of electronic financial services is covered in the following chapter.

# Is it safe?

**2**

Surveys by National Opinion Poll (NOP) show that fewer than half of all UK Internet users believe it is a secure medium for financial transactions. There is also great concern regarding the safety of Internet banking and the number of errors made by e-banks. Among those who have yet to take up any financial services online, nearly six out of ten (59 per cent) think this is an insecure way to buy.

Fears have been fuelled by a number of high-profile security lapses; for example, in July 2000 following an upgrade to the Barclays Bank software, several customers found that when they logged on to their online accounts they could also see the account details of other users of the service. Non-financial companies, such as PowerGen and BT, have had similar problems, as has *Which*? itself. Experts suspect there may be many more incidents that go unreported because firms wish to avoid the bad publicity. There have also been some well-publicised computer crashes, where a firm's computer system has been unable to cope with large numbers of customers. Egg, Cahoot, Intelligent Finance and several online stock-brokers have all been affected.

However, bad news always makes good headlines, so it is important to put these incidents into perspective. What are the real risks when you deal with your finances online, how are you protected and what can you do to make your e-transactions safer?

The laws that protect you when you buy a financial product on the high street or over the phone apply equally when you buy over the Internet. In addition, there are new laws and rules being introduced that focus particularly on the Internet and should help to make it a safer environment.

## The problem of unregulated firms

### *Financial activities regulated by the Financial Services Authority (FSA)*

Before dealing with any financial firm, you need to make sure that it is operating legally, so that you get the benefit of consumer protection.

Most financial products and some types of financial advice come within the scope of the Financial Services Authority (FSA)* – the new super-regulator. Provided a firm is 'authorised' by the FSA, you can be confident that:

- the firm has been checked out to ensure that it is competent, honest and solvent
- in many cases, it must conduct its business according to rules laid down by the FSA concerning, for example, the content of advertisements, the information to be supplied before purchase, the giving of suitable advice, and so on
- there is a proper complaints procedure you can use if something goes wrong, including resort to the Financial Ombudsman Service (FOS),* which from November 2001 absorbs the earlier complaints schemes, such as the Banking Ombudsman and PIA Ombudsman. If the FOS finds in your favour, it can order a firm to pay you compensation up to £100,000
- if you have lost money because of a firm's fraud or negligence, but the firm has gone bust, you may be able to get redress from the Financial Services Compensation Scheme.*

The FSA is due to get its full powers in November 2001, but in the meantime has already taken over most of the day-to-day regulation of financial firms. By law, a firm operating in the UK, whether through the Internet or any other medium, must normally be authorised by the FSA to do any of the following:

- **accept deposits** – a fancy name for offering current accounts and savings accounts (offered, for example, by banks and building societies)

- **offer and administer personal pensions, stakeholder schemes and insurance** – for example, life insurance, income protection, home and motor insurance
- **deal in investments such as shares, corporate bonds, traded options, and so on** – services usually offered by stockbrokers and similar intermediaries
- **manage shares, bonds and so on, and look after them** – for example, a broker or adviser running your share portfolio for you or a broker operating a nominee account
- **offer and run unit trusts, open-ended investment companies (OEICs) or investment trust savings schemes**
- **give advice about investments** – including pensions, life insurance, unit trusts, OEICs, investment trusts, shares, gilts, corporate bonds, traded options, and so on
- **offer or administer mortgages**
- **run a Lloyd's insurance syndicate or give advice about whether you should join a syndicate**.

## UK firms not regulated by the FSA

Some firms are 'appointed representatives' of another firm. An appointed representative does not usually have to be authorised. Instead, the firm it represents – its 'principal' – takes responsibility. Provided the principal is authorised, you get all the normal protection when you deal through the appointed representative.

The mainstream business of solicitors, accountants and actuaries is regulated by the relevant professional body – for example the Law Society in the case of solicitors in England and Wales. The FSA can give a professional body status as a 'designated professional body' (DPB), in which case it can also regulate any of the financial activities listed above if they are incidental to a member firm's mainstream business. For example, a solicitor might safeguard and administer investments as part of the work involved in setting up and running a trust for a client. If a professional's financial activities are *more than* incidental, the firm needs to be authorised by the FSA.

Some financial activities are not regulated by the FSA at all, for example giving advice about general insurance or mortgages. However, there are various voluntary systems that offer you some protection; for example, the General Insurance Standards Council (GISC)* sets out rules of good business conduct for its members (most insurers and intermediaries) and operates an independent complaints procedure. The Mortgage Code Compliance Board (MCCB)* oversees the Mortgage Code, which sets out good practice for mortgage lenders and advisers. There is also an arbitration scheme to deal with mortgage disputes.

## Financial firms based abroad

The Internet lets you search the world from your armchair, so you might be tempted to deal with firms based abroad. But, if you deal with a non-UK firm, you are not protected by the FSA's rules, so you need to check what other safeguards, if any, will protect you if things go wrong.

Firms based in certain other European countries are allowed to operate in the UK without being regulated by the FSA. The countries concerned are the members of the European Economic Area (EEA) and include: Austria, Belgium, Denmark, Finland, France, Germany, Greece, Iceland, Ireland, Italy, Liechtenstein, Luxembourg, the Netherlands, Norway, Portugal, Spain and Sweden. All but Iceland, Liechtenstein and Norway are member states of the European Union (EU).

Instead of falling under the remit of the FSA, EEA firms are controlled by the regulators in their home country. (An example is First-e, a French-based Internet bank operating from Dublin.) The home country (France in the case of First-e) must have provisions to protect consumers. However, these usually differ from the FSA's rules. You need to check whether you are happy with the level of protection before you do business with an EEA firm. In particular you need to check:

- what steps the regulator takes to make sure firms are competent, honest and solvent
- whether there is an independent complaints body. Would you have to make your complaint in a foreign language, or deal with a foreign court system?
- whether there is a compensation scheme.

From March 2002, if you deal with a firm selling to UK customers but based in another EU country, you should be able to pursue any legal action through the UK court system.

Non-EEA firms based overseas cannot legally direct their sales at UK customers or make their promotional material available to people in the UK without authorisation from the FSA. However, this might not stop you buying from an overseas web site, in which case you would be reliant on whatever consumer protection measures – if any – are in place in the country from which the firm operates. Even if there is a formal complaints procedure, you might find it very hard to resolve a dispute; for example, you might have to make your complaint in another language and get to grips with that country's legal system. In general, legal experts suggest that it is rarely economic to pursue a cross-border dispute unless the amount at stake is at least £2,500.

---

## What you can do to protect yourself

- **check whether a firm is regulated** You can find out whether a firm is authorised by the FSA, an appointed representative of an authorised firm, regulated by a DPB or regulated by a regulator in another EEA country by checking the FSA Register* (*www.thecentralregister.co.uk*). You are strongly recommended to check every firm against the Register before you do business with it – see table opposite
- **stick to UK companies** unless you are very confident that you will be covered by adequate, affordable and accessible consumer protection
- **beware of bogus web sites** Some fraudsters set up sites with names very similar to genuine firms, maybe using similar corporate colours and logos too. Be on your guard – if a name is not quite right, for example it is spelt slightly differently, check it carefully against the FSA Register. If you have any doubts, tell the FSA by contacting the FSA Consumer Helpline.*

## Checking the FSA Register

| What the Register says about a firm | What it means | Is it OK to do business with the firm? |
| --- | --- | --- |
| Authorised | Regulated by the FSA.[1] The firm should be sound; there is a complaints procedure and a compensation scheme | Yes |
| EEA authorised | Regulated by the authorities in another EEA country. Similar safeguards to those of the FSA | Yes, but check that you are happy with the level of protection offered by the overseas regulators |
| Exempt (appointed representative) | Acts as a representative for another firm called the 'principal' | Yes, provided you check that the principal is authorised |
| Exempt (member of a designated professional body) | Regulated by a professional body, such as the Law Society or Institute of Chartered Accountants | Yes, but check you are happy with the level of protection provided by the professional body |
| No longer authorised | Used to be regulated, but the firm is no longer open for business | No |
| No entry on the register | The firm is not regulated | No |

1. The FSA takes over regulating firms from November 2001. In the meantime, firms are authorised by one of the regulators the FSA is to replace: Personal Investment Authority (PIA), Securities and Futures Authority (SFA) or Investment Managers Regulatory Organisation (IMRO). After November 2001 you may still see the names of these former regulators on firms' letterheads, brochures and other literature.

## Problems making contact

If everything goes well, you may never need to contact a firm providing goods or services over the Internet in person. But if your credit card or insurance contract does not turn up, by mistake you're billed twice, you can't get the answer to a query at the FAQ site, or you have a complaint or run into any other problems, then you might need to contact the company in writing or by phone. It is therefore essential that any Internet firm you do business with gives a bricks-and-mortar address on its web site, and phone details as well. Be aware that some services designed to be operated over the Internet charge premium rates if you make contact by phone.

---

## What you can do to protect yourself

- before doing business, check the site includes a bricks-and-mortar address and phone number
- print off these contact details and keep them in a safe place
- check the small print to see whether customer support phone lines are charged at a premium rate. Premium-rate numbers start with '09': for example, numbers starting with '0900' or '0901' indicate charges up to 60p a minute, with a total call charge no greater than £5 or a fixed fee up to £1 a call; '0906' indicates an open-ended time-charge or any amount of fixed fee; and '0907' indicates payment for a product costing more than £1.

---

### Problems with security

Before you can buy over a web site, you will be required to give some personal information. Depending on the product you are buying, this might be simply your name and address, or include more detailed information about, for example, your family members, income and existing financial products such as mortgages, pensions and so on. And, if you are paying online, you will be asked for your credit-card details or similar information. You need to be sure that the information you give will reach the web site without interception and will be stored safely once it arrives. A survey by the Department of

Trade and Industry (DTI) found that only one e-trader in seven has a formal security policy.

## Security in transit

Web site browsers have a certain amount of built-in security using 'secure socket layer' (SSL) technology. When you are on a secure site, this converts the information you send into code using a mathematical key – a process called 'encryption'. The information can be decoded only once it has arrived, and then only by the keyholder who has the related mathematical key needed to unlock the information.

It is not impossible for hackers to break the code and access information in transit, but this entails a lot of effort, and, in fact, hacking of this sort is extremely rare. So you can be reasonably confident that, if you are sending information over a secure site, your data is safe.

There are several indicators to look out for to check that you are on a secure site:

- your browser will show a security symbol, usually at the bottom of the screen. With Internet Explorer and Netscape, look for a closed padlock
- the web address will include an 's' after the usual 'http' – so you should see 'https:// followed by the rest of the address
- often your browser will display a message saying you are moving into a secure area.

You should never send sensitive information, such as account or credit-card numbers, by email. Emails are the equivalent of electronic postcards, easily read by anyone. In addition, fraudsters have designed special software that can spot and capture anything contained in an email that looks like a credit-card number.

## Security onsite

It is vital that information a firm has about you is stored securely. Any computer linked to the Internet is open to the world, unless steps are taken to stop anyone deliberately or accidentally peering into its contents. There are two ways a firm can prevent this:

- **use a firewall** Customer information is stored behind a piece of software called a 'firewall' that forces all incoming traffic to stop at a control point where, if the incorrect security responses are given, access is denied
- **store data on a separate computer not linked to the Internet**.

## Security on your own PC

Your own PC is just as vulnerable as any other. Some financial services – for example, some aggregation services (see Chapter 12) – store important information and passwords on your own system. This is not secure unless you have a firewall. Without such a device, viruses designed to send information to other computers could attack your PC.

If you don't have a firewall, you should at least keep up-to-date anti-virus software installed on your PC.

The latest versions of common browsers often give you the option to save user identifications and passwords to avoid keying them in every time you access a site. Storing sensitive information in this way is not safe – you should turn off this option. If you are not sure how to do this, try the Help section on your browser or consult your internet service provider (ISP).

## Security in the post

With some Internet services, you will also be reliant on the post. For example, if you take out an Internet credit card, it is unlikely that you will be able to pick it up at a branch, as these cards are usually sent to you through the post. The Consumer Credit Act 1974 gives you some protection in this situation. You are not liable for use of a credit card until you have signed the card, or signed a receipt for it (unless you – or another authorised user – has already used the card prior to signing it).

## Bogus requests

Some fraud has involved customers being sent emails or receiving phone calls supposedly from an account manager. The bogus manager typically says there has been some problem, and that he or she needs to check your account details. Never give out details by email or phone in response to a request like this. Make your own contact with the account operator using contact details that you know to be genuine, and verify whether there really is a problem. And, whether the call seems genuine or not, never ever give out passwords or personal identification numbers (PINs) – you should always keep these to yourself.

---

## What you can do to protect yourself

- check a firm's security policy before doing business and print off a copy of the policy
- if you can't find a security policy, email the firm to request a copy or details of how the firm handles security. If the firm is unable to supply a security policy, think twice about doing business with it
- only send personal information and payment details over a secure site
- never email sensitive information
- don't give out account information unless you are certain you are giving it to someone who is authorised to know these details. Report any suspicious requests for information to the FSA*
- never reveal your passwords or PINs.

---

### Privacy problems

You need to be confident that information you give a firm will not be misused. The Data Protection Act 1998 gives you certain rights:

- data on you should not be processed unless you have given your consent, or unless the processing is necessary for a contract to go ahead, for legal reasons, to carry out public functions, and so on
- data should be processed lawfully and fairly. This includes collecting data without deceiving or misleading you about

the purpose for which the data will be used. You should be told who is collecting the data and how it will be used
- data should be processed only for limited purposes. In other words, having gathered data about you for a particular purpose, the firm is not allowed to use it for some other different purpose as well
- data should be accurate. This includes, where relevant, keeping it up to date
- data should be adequate, relevant and not excessive
- data should not be retained for longer than necessary
- data should be processed only in accordance with your rights. For example, you have the right to see data held about you, and you have the right to prevent the data being used for direct marketing
- data should be held securely. The firm must take steps to protect the data from being destroyed or misused – for example, keeping data safe from Internet hackers and making sure staff are trustworthy
- data should not be transferred to countries outside the EEA that do not offer adequate protection.

Firms that breach these conditions are breaking the law and can be fined. However, despite this, surveys suggest that fewer than half of e-traders comply with the Act. You can be awarded compensation if you suffer loss as a result of a breach.

In a survey for the Information Commissioner* (formerly the Data Protection Commissioner), 77 per cent of people in the UK said they were concerned about the amount of data being held on them, and 72 per cent were concerned about organisations' lack of openness with regard to their handling of data. To combat this, firms that gather data about you are being encouraged to use a new 'information padlock'. Not to be confused with the closed padlock symbol that indicates a secure site (see page 23), the information padlock has a lowercase letter 'i' on it and can be any colour. Participating firms agree to show the padlock wherever data are being collected and to use it to signpost you to an explanation of why the information is requested.

All web sites should contain a privacy statement telling you that the site collects information about you, if this is the case, and what data are collected, why they are collected and how they will be used. The statement should also tell you whether the site uses 'cookies' – bits of software containing data (such as your user name and maybe your preferences) that the site places on your own computer so that next time you visit the site it can be customised for you.

---

## What you can do to protect yourself

- check the firm's privacy statement before you supply any information and print off a copy of the statement
- if you can't find a privacy statement, email a request for a copy. If the firm does not provide a privacy statement, think twice about dealing with this firm
- if you are unhappy about web sites placing cookies on your computer, you can stop this by changing your browser options. For advice on how to do this, visit *www.cookiecentral.com*

---

## Problems with terms and conditions

Before taking out any financial product, check the terms and conditions. This is especially important in the case of services to be delivered over the Net, such as banking.

In particular, watch out for any terms that try to make you liable for things outside your control. For example, some Internet banks hold you liable for all money taken out of your account through unauthorised withdrawals made before you notify the bank of a possible security breach. By the time you've spotted the breach, you could have lost a great deal of money.

Also take care to check what happens if you want to cancel a service or withdraw from an investment – are there any penalties?

Make sure you print off a copy of the terms and conditions and any other information on which you have based a decision to buy – for example, the key features document for an investment. It is very easy for firms to alter their terms and conditions on the Internet. If you go back onsite later to check something, you may find that the terms are no longer the same as those you had agreed to.

Finally, keep a copy of any email from the firm, for example confirming the deal you have just done or advising of changes to terms and conditions.

---

## What you can do to protect yourself

- read the terms and conditions before signing up
- if any term seems unreasonable, think twice about taking up that product or service and tell *Which?*\* about it
- print off the terms and conditions and any other information or messages relating to the deal. (If you can't see a 'print' button on your screen, right-click the mouse and select 'print'.) Keep the information in a safe place.

---

## Payment problems

If you are buying, say, insurance over the Internet, using a credit card or debit card is an obvious way to pay. But surveys show that consumers still worry about using their credit card online, though confidence has been improving steadily. Around a quarter of UK Internet users have given their credit-card details over the Net. The proportion is much higher (79 per cent) among the 20 per cent or so of users who shop online.

### *Paying with a credit card or debit card*

Consumers' main fear is that their card details will be intercepted and misused. But using your credit or debit card over the Internet is no less safe than using it over the phone, in a shop or in a restaurant. Provided you are giving the details over a secure site (see page 23), using your card online may even be safer because your card information is encrypted and only unscrambled on arrival.

There are many ways in which fraudsters operate, but it is rare for card details to be stolen online. Cards may be 'skimmed' in restaurants, hotels and shops, which involves taking a copy of the details on the face of a card during the course of a genuine transaction. The details are then used for purchases by phone or Internet (called 'cardholder-not-present' transactions) or can be put on to a counterfeit card. Fraudsters also get card numbers from discarded receipts in, say, supermarket trolleys and car parks. Some fraudsters are able to crack the system that issuers use to generate card numbers, and so create their own valid numbers.

Online card fraud amounted to £7 million in 2000 – only a small fraction of the £300 million total card fraud. The losers are usually the retailers rather than the consumers. Typically, a fraudster will buy goods from a web site using stolen card details, the genuine cardholder disputes the item on his or her bill, the card issuer cancels the item and then seeks the money from the retailer – called a 'chargeback' – on the basis that the retailer should have done more to verify that the card user was genuine. The true cardholder is protected. Since 31 October 2000, European legislation, called the Distance Selling Directive, has come into force in the UK. The aim of this legislation is to give consumers better protection when they are shopping by phone, Internet and mail order. One of the provisions is that consumers cannot be held liable for any unauthorised use of their payment cards.

Unfortunately, the Distance Selling Directive does not apply to purchases of financial goods and services, although a separate directive due to be implemented in 2002 will cover these. In the meantime, your liability for unlawful use of your credit or debit card to buy financial goods and services is limited to a maximum of £50 before you have notified the card authorities – and even this is often waived. Once you have notified the card issuer, you are not liable at all (unless you have been dishonest or negligent).

Although online card fraud is not currently a major problem, the banks are keen to pre-empt its growth and to reassure consumers that the Internet is a safe environment for shopping and financial transactions. Various measures are in train; for example, since April 2001, when you use your card by phone, Internet or post, you should be asked for a three-digit security number from the signature strip on the back of the card and your address, as well as giving the usual card details.

Card issuers are replacing magnetic-stripe technology with smart cards that carry a microchip. The chip can store a large amount of data including digital certificates and digital signatures that uniquely identify the cardholder. One possibility is that, in future, you might have a small card reader that you plug into your computer (or perhaps eventually it will be built into computers as a standard feature). When you wanted to make an online purchase, you would swipe your card in the reader and the necessary details would be sent directly from reader to retailer. American Express has already adopted this system, issuing free smart-card readers to some of its US cardholders. The strength of the system lies in turning a cardholder-not-present transaction into a card-present transaction, immediately putting a stop to some types of fraud.

Even more fraud could be stamped out if transactions could, in effect, be turned from cardholder-not-present to cardholder-present. This would involve verifying the user's identity in some way. You could be asked to provide a PIN or password that the card issuer checks before a transaction goes ahead. Eventually, you might have a digital certificate or digital signature stored in an electronic wallet that is able to communicate with your PC (and other equipment such as your mobile phone). This might involve plugging the wallet into the PC or, perhaps, a wireless transmission using 'Bluetooth', an international standard for short-range wireless that could eventually do away with the spaghetti of wires behind most electronic equipment.

## Alternative ways to pay

If you are still not convinced that paying online by credit card is safe, you could consider an alternative means of electronic payment, such as 'purse cards' (like Splash Plastic) and 'shield' systems (like Securicor's Safedoor). These are described in Chapter 16. Or, sometimes, you can resort to a cheque in the post.

However, bear in mind that when you pay for goods by credit card you get extra protection under the Consumer Credit Act 1974, provided the goods or services cost more than £100 but no more than £30,000. If anything goes wrong, you can claim redress from either the provider of the goods or the credit-card issuer. If you pay by some other means (including a debit card) you do not benefit from this protection.

---

# What you can do to protect yourself

- only give card details over a secure connection
- never send card details by email
- dispose of card receipts carefully
- always check card statements and query anything unusual
- stop your card immediately if you suspect it is being misused.

---

## Codes of practice

TrustUK* is an organisation that promotes high standards of Internet trading and allows its hallmark to be used where an e-trader has agreed to abide by a code of practice that meets TrustUK's standards. The standards are designed to:

- protect your privacy by ensuring that the firm complies with the requirements of the Data Protection Act 1998 (see page 25)
- ensure that your payments are secure
- help you to make an informed decision to buy
- let you know what you have agreed to and how to cancel the deal
- ensure that goods or services are delivered within a specified time (30 days, unless you have agreed some other time limit)
- protect children
- sort out any complaints.

At the time of writing, three codes of practice had received TrustUK approval: the Association of British Travel Agents, the Direct Marketing Association and Which? Web Trader.* The full Which? Web Trader code of practice is set out in Appendix I.

For a list of financial firms that have signed up to the Which? Web Trader code, see Appendix II. To check the most up-to-date list, visit *www.which.net/webtrader*. Firms on the list have agreed to follow the guidelines drawn up by Which?, but inclusion on the list does NOT mean that Which? or its associated companies in any way endorse or recommend the firm's products or services. And be aware that the code applies only to the traders' web sites, not to any other activities the firm is engaged in.

## How to buy financial products safely on the Internet

- check the FSA Register to make sure the firm is regulated
- stick to UK companies unless you are happy with the protection offered by the overseas regulator
- beware of bogus web sites. Check details carefully against the FSA Register
- make sure the site gives a bricks-and-mortar address and telephone number. Print off a copy of these details
- check whether customer support lines are charged at premium rates (starting '09')
- check the web site's security policy. Print off a copy
- check the site's privacy policy. Print off a copy
- read the terms and conditions. Print off a copy
- print off other information on which you have based your choice – for example key features documents, brochures and details of special offers
- only give personal information over a secure site – look for the closed padlock
- only give credit-card or other payment details over a secure site – look for the closed padlock
- look for the TrustUK or Which? Web Trader logo.

# The advantages of e-finance

## 3

Hype about the Internet would have you believe we will eventually be transacting all our financial affairs at the touch of a button or click of a mouse. But e-finance will only catch on if it offers you, the consumer, real advantages over traditional transactions and if these are enough to compensate for the concerns outlined in Chapter 2.

## Convenience

A big plus point with any form of 'distance buying' – in other words, buying by phone, post or Internet – is that you don't have to traipse out to a shop or branch to do business. You can, say, buy insurance, handle your bank account or invest in an individual savings account (ISA) from the comfort of your own home.

Unlike phone services, the Internet also has the advantage that you can usually do business any time of day or night, any day of the year.

## Access

Being able to do business from your own home is an enormous advantage for anyone who finds it hard to get out – for example, if you are disabled or have young children at home. It is also a great boon if you are simply pressed for time or have the type of job where it is hard to take time out to handle your personal affairs.

Distance buying can also bring services to remote areas that would otherwise have to go without. An extreme example is the island of St Helena, a British dependency in the middle of the Atlantic (and famous as the final home of the exiled

Napoleon I). For decades its businesses were forced to use a primitive savings bank operated by the island's government, or rely on fax and post to deal with banks in the UK. In 2000 an Internet bank was launched in St Helena and is expected to revolutionise the island's economy.

Closer to home, e-finance can bring services to, say, rural areas that are geographically remote from conventional banks.

It might also bring services to people who are remote from financial services for other reasons. The so-called 'financially excluded' are people who typically do not have bank accounts, buy insurance or build up savings, often because their income or credit record puts these services out of reach. The exclusion can also arise for more complex reasons – a cultural background that puts faith in the cash economy and lacks confidence in dealing with institutions, such as banks. But these groups, along with the rest of the population, are generally comfortable with the medium of television and are often already experienced with distance shopping, for example buying by catalogue or in response to TV shopping channels. Therefore, if digital TV becomes the norm, as has been predicted, in the long run it might be a relatively small step for these groups to take up, say, e-banking or e-insurance via the TV.

## Speed

In theory, the Internet offers the potential for transactions to be made more rapidly than they can be at a branch, where it may be necessary to queue. And, because of its 24-hour accessibility, you may be able to leave transactions to the last minute.

Theory is one thing; practice is not always so straightforward. Although the technology is becoming increasingly reliable, computers do crash, web pages can, for seemingly inexplicable reasons, be unavailable, and you can even be jinxed by a fault on your phone line. So if, for example, you have left sending in your tax return or using your ISA allowance to the last possible day, these kinds of problems can be more than just frustrating; they can cost you hard cash if you incur a penalty or miss out on a tax relief.

Another problem is that currently Internet transactions are often not completely e-based. Many still rely on old-fashioned paper-based systems. For example, having found your perfect ISA on 5 April (the last day of the tax year), you may well then discover you have to print out the application form and send it through the post. The same goes for credit cards and loans – until new regulations are brought into force, you must physically sign an agreement, which means it is impossible to complete the whole transaction online.

## Saving money

Competition among firms supplying goods and services over the Internet is often intense, particularly among banks and share-dealing services. As long as these firms are fighting for your custom, there are often some very good deals to be had. For example, the chart overleaf shows the interest rates available with different types of instant-access and no-notice savings accounts in May 2001. The traditional branch-based accounts tended to offer the lowest returns, with many paying only 1 or 2 per cent a year. The majority of Internet accounts offered between 4 and 6 per cent a year. Many postal and phone-based accounts were also in this range. However, the very highest rates on the market were offered by Internet-only accounts.

The Internet can deliver competitive deals in other ways too. In 2000, Money Supermarket (*www.moneysupermarket. com*) introduced mortgage auctions in the UK. Instead of shopping around for the best deal, you enter your details and a panel of mortgage lenders bids to provide you with a loan (see Chapter 9 for more details). This may make it possible for you to attract a better deal than a normal off-the-shelf mortgage.

Selling by Internet (or phone or post) can give financial providers big cost savings that could be passed on to customers. If the alternative is selling through a branch, the provider can save the cost of a branch network; if the alternative is selling through a sales rep visiting your home or office, the provider saves the cost of running a sales force. In February 2001, Prudential made the headlines by announcing

## Return on £1,000 offered by different types of instant-access and no-notice savings accounts[1]

*The chart shows the number of accounts of each type offering interest rates in the range shown by the axis on the left.*

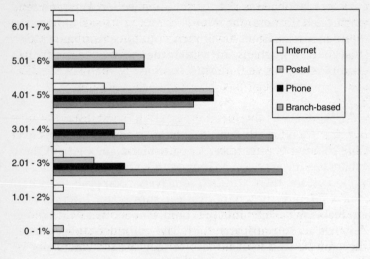

Number of accounts of offered

1. Excludes accounts not available nationally
Based on data from *Moneyfacts*, May 2001.

that its insurance sales force ('the man from the Pru') was to be axed and replaced by phone and Internet.

The Internet can also be cheaper than phone-based selling, saving the cost of staffing a large call centre. A survey in 1999 suggested that the cost of a banking transaction was €1 in a bank branch, €0.5 by phone, €0.25 at a cash machine and just €0.12 via an Internet site. But figures like these can be misleading, because they cover only the direct cost of the transaction itself.

Some experts believe that Internet products will not necessarily be best buys in the long run. Although setting up a web site may be inexpensive compared with opening a string of bricks-and-mortar branches, and although the cost of each web-based transaction may be tiny, a provider of goods and services over the Internet still has to attract customers. The cost of promoting a new Internet brand can be enormous, with no guarantee that costly advertising will produce the desired volume of customers. For example, in 2000, Marbles, an online credit-card company, cut back on mainstream advertising because it was costing £250 to attract each new customer, which was simply uneconomic. And, perversely, while bricks-and-mortar 'Pru' is shedding its sales force, its Internet protégé Egg is looking at developing a string of high-street outlets, perhaps through Prudential-owned shopping centres or a joint venture with an existing high-street retail chain – a move Egg has described as developing a 'skinny branch network'.

So, for now, the Internet has some of the best deals around, but don't assume this will necessarily always be the case. Check out other ways to buy and invest too.

## Simplicity

Products available by Internet or phone are often deliberately designed to be transparent and easy to understand, so that they can be sold with little or no advice. This simplicity is particularly welcome in the case of products that are some-times complicated in their traditional form. For example, some unit trusts sold over the Internet or phone have simplified charges, with just an annual fee instead of the annual fee plus bid–offer spread more common with conventional unit trusts.

## Control

If you are put off buying or investing by the thought of several hours' patter from an eager salesperson, the Internet offers a number of advantages as an alternative. You can surf for infor-mation, make your own decisions and send in your appli-cation without a sales rep in sight. Instead of having to sift out the facts from the sales hype, you can focus on the key infor-mation that is important to you. Instead of being pressured into signing up here and now – 'otherwise, you'll miss this special opportunity' – you can take your time to consider a deal and compare it with other products.

In other words, the Internet puts you in control of the buying process. The downside is that it also puts you in control of making your own mistakes. Several Internet sites are beginning to introduce online financial advice, but on the whole buying via the Internet means buying without advice. Any errors of judgement are yours alone, so you cannot complain or seek redress if the product turns out to be wrong for you.

It pays to do your homework before you buy: for example background reading on the type of product – what it does, its suitability for you, typical cost, features to look out for and pitfalls to avoid. Sources to consider include books (for example, *Be Your Own Financial Adviser*, the *Which? Guide to Insurance* and *Which? Way to Save and Invest*, all published by Which? Books*), regular personal finance articles in *Which? Magazine*, personal finance magazines such *as Money Management* and *Moneywise*, and the money sections of newspapers and web sites. Chapters 5 to 15 include web sites that are particularly helpful as sources of background information.

In summary, the Internet is ideal for consumers who like to shop around for themselves and are confident making their own decisions.

## Confidence

If you have only limited knowledge or experience of money matters, you may find financial transactions quite daunting. A survey in 1995 by Janet Levin Associates revealed that inexperienced consumers often lacked the confidence to ask questions and were fearful of seeming foolish. Many preferred buying at a distance – for example, by post – because of the privacy this affords. For the same reasons, inexperienced and less confident consumers may be drawn to the Internet, despite the fact that these consumers are among those who are probably most likely to benefit from financial advice. Without help from an adviser, there is a high risk that these consumers will buy an unsuitable product.

If you don't feel confident about financial matters, the Internet may not be the best way for you to buy – at least for now. Build up your background knowledge first, and consider getting advice from one or two independent advisers. (See Chapter 13 for how to find an adviser.)

## Managing your finances

Computers make it easy for you to manage your budget or keep track of your finances. There are many software packages available – see Chapter 4 for details of the market leaders. Linking your software to the Internet is an obvious step that lets you, for example, access up-to-date share prices to value your portfolio or download your latest bank statement into your budgeting software.

Many Internet sites offer handy calculators, for example to calculate your monthly mortgage repayments, work out the cost of a loan or show how much you have to save to reach a given target. These can also help you handle your finances more easily.

## The Internet as an information tool

The Internet is a vast reservoir of information on all sorts of topics. When it comes to your finances, you can really turn this to your advantage. For example, if you want to buy and sell shares, your daily newspaper will list only yesterday's closing prices – it does not tell you how much you will get or pay if you sell or buy today. But the Internet can deliver up-to-the-minute dealing prices to your PC. There was a time when private investors were starved of much of the information they needed to make sensible choices about share dealing. Now analysts' reports, price charts, ratios and more are available on the Web.

Shopping around for a mortgage, say, used to be a chore, and you probably gave up after visiting half a dozen lenders. Now, in minutes, you can easily find a suitable deal from maybe thousands of mortgages listed on a single web site. And if you want to check a tax point or work out what pension you can expect from the state, you no longer need to trail off to a tax office or Benefits Agency.

As well as bald information, many web sites include flow-charts and calculators to guide you through your choices.

The Internet can empower you as a consumer by giving you the necessary information to make the right choices.

# The Which? Guide to Money on the Internet

## Pros and cons of the Internet compared with other ways of buying or investing

|  | Internet | Branch | Phone | Post |
|---|---|---|---|---|
| You do not need any special equipment | ✗ | ✓ | ✓ | ✓ |
| No limited opening hours | ✓ | ✗ | Maybe | ✓ |
| You can shop from home | ✓ | ✗ | ✓ | ✓ |
| It is easy to shop around lots of providers | ✓ | ✗ | ✓ | ✗ |
| It is easy to find extra information | ✓ | ✗ | Maybe | ✗ |
| Speedy transactions are possible | ✓ | Maybe | ✓ | ✗ |
| Technical problems are rare | ✗ | ✓ | ✓ | ✓ |
| You can often save money or get a better deal | ✓ | ✗ | ✓ | ✓ |
| Products are often very straightforward | ✓ | ✗ | ✓ | ✗ |
| You do not have to deal with salespeople | ✓ | ✗ | Maybe | ✓ |
| You usually get the benefit of advice | ✗ | ✓ | Maybe | ✗ |

# Getting started

4

Before you can handle your finances online, you need to get connected to the Internet. At present, the main way to do this is via a computer, although other ways of doing so are explored later in this chapter.

## Connecting to the Internet using a computer

To get on to the Internet you need:

- a computer
- an adaptor to link your computer to a phone line
- a phone line
- an account with an internet service provider (ISP)
- appropriate software.

If you don't have your own equipment, many libraries now have Internet facilities that you can use for a fee – for example, £3 an hour. Some schools open their computers to public use, say, in the evenings. Cybercafés (cafés and restaurants with Internet facilities for hire) are also springing up all over the place. Accessing the Internet via any of these ways is great if you are already reasonably competent – if not, it's a good idea to get some basic training first, for example through an evening class at your local community education centre.

When it comes to e-finance, access via a library, school or cybercafé is fine if you are searching for information or a good deal. However, this would be a cumbersome way of running a bank account or share-dealing service, say, and services of this type often insist for security reasons that you use a computer you do not share with other people.

## A computer

Any computer from around 1993 onwards should be capable of handling the Internet, but you'll get the best results if your machine runs Windows 95 or above if you're using a PC, or System 7.5 or above if you're using an Apple Mac.

If you want to connect to the Internet using Asymmetric Digital Subscriber Line (ADSL – see opposite), you'll generally need a 1995-onwards computer.

Note that the more powerful your machine, the better your experience of the Internet is likely to be.

## An adaptor to link your computer to a phone line

### Using an existing phone line

You need a modem (**mo**dulator-**dem**odulator) to turn the digital language your computer speaks into the sounds the phone line can transmit.

There are two types of modem: internal and external. If your computer came with an internal modem already fitted, well and good. If not, an external modem will often be the better choice.

An external modem is a stand-alone box that you plug into your computer. It is easy to install, and a display on the front of the box tells you when you are online and transmitting or receiving information.

Internal modems are circuit cards that slot inside your computer. They are notoriously difficult to set up and get working and a suitable choice only if you have some technical expertise with computer hardware.

The speed of your modem will determine how rapidly you can send and receive information via the Internet, so you need to choose one that is reasonably fast. Prices have been coming down and, as a result, the slowest modems are tending to vanish from the market. The industry standard is what is called a '56k' modem. This lets you download data at speeds up to

57.6 thousand bits per second (kbps – usually abbreviated to 'k'). In fact, because of the limitations of phone lines, the average download speed is usually around 42k, and the speed at which you can send information is limited to 33.6k.

You can usually pick up a 56k modem for between £50 and £150. If you are buying an external modem, you may need an adaptor to fit the appropriate port on your computer.

## Integrated Services Digital Network (ISDN)

ISDN (see overleaf) is a faster service that sends digital infor-mation down your phone line. Because the phone line and computer are speaking the same language, you do not need a modem. However, you will need an external ISDN adaptor or internal ISDN card. As with modems, the external adaptor is easier to set up and install.

## Asymmetric Digital Subscriber Line (ADSL)

The provider of the ADSL service (see page 45) will sort out the equipment you need.

## A phone line

### Your ordinary BT phone line

The most common way to access the internet is via your ordinary phone line. This has the advantages of being inex-pensive and simple to use. On the minus side:

- your connection will be relatively slow, which means that it can take a long time for web sites to download, espe-cially if they have a lot of graphics (non-text) material
- your connection will be 'intermittent', meaning you have to dial up to access the Internet and then hang up when you're finished. To be permanently connected would be very expensive and, in any case, most ISPs hang up on users whose connections have been inactive for a while
- you can't use your phone for ordinary calls while you are online, unless you have a second phone line
- ordinary phone lines can be unreliable.

Despite these drawbacks, connecting over your ordinary phone line is, for now, the most sensible option for most people. BT offers a variety of payment packages, some of which are especially designed for people who expect to use the Internet a lot.

## A second phone line

You can restore your ability to make and receive ordinary phone calls at the same time as you are online by installing a second phone line. A word of warning though: make sure BT does not simply install a DACS box. This combines two phone lines into one and is fine if you are using both lines for ordinary voice calls, however Internet access over either of these lines will be frustratingly slow. You may have to be very insistent with BT to get a genuinely separate second line installed.

BT makes special offers from time to time, but in June 2001 the standard cost of a second line was £99. You will also have to pay a second quarterly rental, which at the time was £29.97 at the standard rate.

## ISDN

ISDN works by converting your phone line into a digital connection. Your line is split into two, each capable of receiving data at up to 64k. You can use one line for voice calls and the other for the Internet. You can also link the two lines so that you are using both simultaneously as an Internet connection, with speeds up to 128k, though you will have to pay double the call charge.

The higher ISDN speed means that you can access web pages much faster than using an ordinary phone link. And, because the connection is digital, you do not lose time and quality converting the digital signals to sound, as is the case with a modem. This means that you should be able to connect to the Internet more quickly and have the benefit of a more reliable service.

The drawback with ISDN is cost. BT offers several ISDN services. The most appropriate service for residential users is called Home Highway. In June 2001, the standard charge for Home Highway was £175.08 to convert your existing line to

ISDN, and £27 a month rental. But you could opt for other packages, for example a £49.50 conversion charge plus £39.99 a month rental including up to £13 of calls.

ISDN is available throughout most of Britain but not in remote rural areas.

## *ADSL*

ADSL provides an even faster digital connection than ISDN using 'broadband' technology. Typically ADSL transmits and receives information at speeds up to ten times faster than a modem. This makes for rapid download of web pages and also makes it feasible to view films or listen to music over the Net.

ADSL provides a permanent ('always on') connection to the Internet for a flat fee. BT supplies ADSL direct to customers through its subsidiary BTopenworld, and also acts as a wholesale supplier of ADSL facilities to other providers, such as Freeserve.

In 2001, BTopenworld was charging £150 to covert you to ADSL and £39.99 a month rental. Other providers may charge more, largely, they say, because of the high price BT charges them for the ADSL facilities. For example, in May 2001 Freeserve announced that it was increasing its charges to a £170 conversion fee plus £49.99 a month rental (in other words, nearly £600 a year). Typically, you have to sign up to the service for at least a year.

ADSL can only be provided where local phone exchanges have been converted to handle the service. By October 2000, 619 exchanges had been converted covering 40 per cent of homes and businesses, mainly in urban areas. Some cable companies offer their own version of ADSL to subscribers, usually for around £50 a month.

The government has a target of giving the whole nation access to broadband services like ADSL by 2005, though this aim is surrounded by controversy. Surveys suggest that consumers are willing to pay only around £10 a month for broadband services. Certainly at £600 a year, ADSL is unlikely to become a mass-market product. Conversion of the remaining BT exchanges is now likely to be slow or non-existent. So, unless you are in an area that can already access

ADSL, it is doubtful that this option will be open to you in the near future. You can check whether you are in an ADSL area by visiting the BTopenworld web site (*www.btopenworld.com*).

## An account with an ISP

An ISP is a firm that provides you with a gateway to the Internet. If you opt for ISDN or ADSL, you will be restricted to a small range of ISPs that accept these types of connection. If you are using a modem over your ordinary phone line, there are literally hundreds of ISPs to choose from. Factors you should take into account are:

- cost
- content
- speed of access
- reliability
- support
- free software
- terms and conditions.

### Cost

Many ISPs offer free trials letting you test their service before you commit. Usually you have to provide your credit-card details upfront, so you need to make sure you cancel any service you decide not to go ahead with. If you do stick with the ISP, once the free trial is over you usually have to pay.

There is a vast range of charging options, for example you can:

- pay by the minute for Internet access and for call charges
- pay a fixed monthly fee for Internet access (which might be unlimited or limited to a maximum number of hours per month) plus call charges.
- pay just for call charges with free Internet access
- have free calls and free Internet access (called 'unmetered access').

The first option – paying by the minute for both calls and Internet access – could work out very expensive and is best avoided. Beware if you sign up for a free trial – at the end of the trial you may go automatically on to a pay-by-the-minute service unless you actively choose another option.

The last option – free calls and free access – is not always quite what it seems. The ISP has to make its money from somewhere, and there are several catches to watch out for. For example, there might be a one-off charge when you first sign up. In exchange you get free, lifetime access, but bear in mind that this will last for the lifetime of the ISP – which could be short – rather than your lifetime. The ISP might make its money from advertisers, so your screen could be cluttered with lots of ads that you can't turn off. A condition of the free service might be that you switch your phone line from BT to another phone company and, say, agree to spend a certain amount per month on calls. You'll need to weigh up whether the phone company deal would cost you more than you are saving on the free ISP.

Probably the most common charging model is free Internet access where you pay only for call charges. Calls to your ISP are almost always charged at the local rate wherever you live, and the ISP receives part of what you are paying for the calls.

Given all the lower-cost options, if you choose an ISP that charges a monthly fee, you need to be satisfied that the fee is justified by the ISP's content, superior speed, better technical support or more useful software package.

## *Content*

Many ISPs (sometimes called 'access providers') provide just a bare gateway to the Internet. Others (called 'content providers') have all sorts of extras on their web site that are available only to their members. Content providers are more likely than access providers to charge users a monthly fee but some charge you only for calls.

Typically, content providers bring together in one place information that they think might be useful to their users – for example news digest, travel information, links to shopping sites and so on. They also offer chatrooms and newsgroups. Some, such as Which? Online,* offer specialist information not available on other sites.

47

A content provider can be a good choice if you are new to the Internet and would find it useful to be signposted to web sites on particular topics. If you are more experienced or confident, you may prefer an access-only ISP.

## Speed

The speed at which you can download web pages depends on all sorts of factors: for example, your modem (see page 42), the amount and type of information on the web page (graphics and photographs tend to be slow), and the number of people trying to look at a web site at the same time as you (this varies, in particular with the time of day). But an important factor is the speed at which your ISP links to the rest of the Internet.

*Which?* Magazine* tested 24 ISPs in 1999. A special computer program timed how long it took each ISP to download a number of different web pages. The testing went on 24 hours a day over a period of three months and came up with real differences in speed between the fastest and slowest ISPs. For example, on a weekday evening, the fastest ISP would download a page from an electronic newspaper (text and pictures) in about nine seconds, which was less than half the time taken by the slowest ISP.

Finding out about speed is no simple matter. You could sign up for lots of free trials and compare the speed of competing ISPs. However this is cumbersome. First, you'll need to remember to cancel those ISPs that you decide against, otherwise you could start to run up charges once the free trial ends. Second, the software provided by one ISP is not always compatible with the software of another, so trying to run several ISP accounts at once could cause glitches.

Your best bet is to look in the specialist magazines that you'll find on most newsagents' shelves. Many magazines run regular or occasional surveys of ISPs, and the better surveys should include some guidance on speed.

## Reliability

Some ISPs are permanently overloaded and unable to cope with the volume of people who want to use their service at any one time. This will affect the speed at which you can download web pages and also your ability to get online at all.

When you connect to your ISP, typically information from your computer is converted by modem to sounds that are then converted back to digital signals by a modem linked to your ISP's computer. Success in getting a connection to your ISP is directly related to the number of modems your ISP has and to the number of people trying to log on at any one time. A ratio of five users to one modem is acceptable, and the average is around ten users per modem. However, some ISPs work on ratios as high as 30 users per modem, and this will mean you often get the busy tone instead of a connection.

Another point to bear in mind is that, if your ISP is running thousands of modems, there are bound at any time to be some that are not working properly. In this case, your computer's call will be answered but you'll still fail to log on (and, annoyingly, you'll be paying for this failed call). If the ISP doesn't have a good system for identifying and repairing faulty modems, the service will be unreliable.

In general, you should expect to log on at your first attempt. There's nothing to worry about if occasionally you have to try two or three times. But, if you're regularly dialling up ten times before you get a connection, it's time to look for another ISP.

## Support

Unfortunately, given the relative newness of the Internet, you would be very lucky not to encounter any problems, and it's important that you can turn to a good support service when you do.

Before signing up to an ISP, it's worth making a test call to its support service to see what sort of response you get.

- a good service should not assume you have any technical knowledge and should be able to walk you through your problem. If all you get is a stream of unintelligible gobbledegook, choose another ISP
- check when support is available – is it a 24-hour service or available only during limited hours?
- watch out for high call charges to the support service. Free

Internet services in particular often charge up to £1 a minute for support
- send in a problem and see how long it takes to get a reply. Bear in mind that email support is not accessible if your problem is that you are unable to make a connection.

## Terms and conditions

- check out the small print before you sign up. In particular, are you committed to staying with the same ISP for a minimum period of time? If you are connecting using an ISDN or ADSL service, you usually have to sign up for a year at a time
- what is the ISP's privacy policy – will it pass your information on to third parties? You should, by law, be given the opportunity to refuse this
- check whether there are restrictions on your use of the service. For example, one free ISP allowed connection 24 hours a day but restricted users to just ten minutes per session, after which they were cut off.

## Other factors

Depending on the use you intend to make of the Internet, you might be attracted by extras such as:

- free web space, so you can publish your own web site
- multiple or unlimited email addresses – for example so that each family member can have their own address.

Beware of bogus ISPs that advertise only on the Internet and give no bricks-and-mortar address or phone number. Typically, these providers invite you to enter your details and supply email details of friends who might also sign up. You're told the ISP will be up and running shortly, once a technical problem has been resolved. But the ISP is never launched and the email lists are sold to firms that send out junk emails ('spam').

## Appropriate software

All ISPs provide at least the basics – a browser to let you
explore the Internet and some sort of email facility. The most
common web browsers are Microsoft Internet Explorer and
Netscape Navigator.

It is useful to have software that allows you to read and
write emails while you are offline.

Once you are linked to the Internet you can search for web
sites from which you can download other software to enhance
your system.

### *Financial management software*

You might be using commercial software to help you organise
your finances. The two leading products are Microsoft Money
and Intuit Quicken. Both use links with the Internet to
enhance their banking and investment systems, and to
provide some other information. This sort of crossover
between software installed on your PC and the resources
available on the Internet is more developed in the US than in
the UK but is likely to become more common in the future.

Typically, commercial software lets you perform some or all
of the functions below:

- **budgeting** Maintaining a log of income and expenses,
  analysing where your money goes
- **debt management** Helping you to prioritise spending
- **payment of bills** Alerting you when bills are due, automatically logging bills that are paid by standing order or
  direct debit
- **banking** Tracking payments into and out of your
  account, helping you to reconcile your account with bank
  statements. The software may also let you link directly to
  an online bank account to automatically register
  payments and download statements straight into your
  money-management system
- **savings accounts** Tracking payments into and out of
  your accounts
- **investments** Maintaining one or more accounts with
  details of your shares, investment trusts, unit trusts and so

on, and tracking the value of each holding. If you enter a share's 'ticker code' (a stock market code assigned to each quoted company), the software will automatically download the latest price when you go online. You can usually also download quotes for unit trusts and open-ended investment companies (OEICs).

Other facilities you might get in a standard package are mortgage tracking and creating an inventory of your belongings for home insurance purposes. In more advanced packages (which cost more), you might also get tax software to help you complete your self-assessment tax return, planning tools (for example to compare the cost of different mortgages or decide how much you need to save for retirement) and will-writing guidance. Some versions help you handle business accounts as well as your personal finances. Other online options include being able to view up-to-date articles on money topics.

In March 2000, *Which?* asked five readers to test-drive the standard versions of Microsoft Money and Intuit Quicken, and its experts assessed the packages. The verdict was that there was little to choose between these two market leaders. The experts thought Intuit Quicken gave more help with tax and mortgages, but more of the users preferred Microsoft Money mainly because of its layout (which is similar to other Microsoft programs and uses standard buttons that you find on a web browser) and ease of use.

Whether or not you want to use money-management software for budgeting and tracking accounts is very much a matter of personal preference. You can do the same job using a pen and paper or a spreadsheet program (such as Excel). When it comes to investments, again you could use a spread-sheet together with a portfolio tracker, such as those you can find on many general personal finance web sites and share-dealing web sites.

Some of the analysis tools can be very useful – for example, working out the cost of a mortgage or other loan, or calcu-lating what you need to save now to achieve a desired pension. But again, many web sites have similar tools available for any visitor to use.

Where commercial software often comes into its own is in

helping you to fill in your tax return and minimise your tax bill (see Chapter 14).

## Other ways to link to the Net

### *Digital TV*

If you have digital TV, you also have the option of using inter-active services, including banking and buying insurance. The government sees digital TV as an important way to access the Internet and promote e-commerce. It has a target of switching the whole nation to digital TV between 2006 and 2010. However, consumers seem less enthusiastic.

Digital TV first became available towards the end of 1998. Initial take-up was rapid, with 21 per cent (5 million) of UK homes having digital TV by August 2000, according to a survey carried out by NOP for telecommunications regulator Oftel. However, apart from playing games, only around one in ten digital viewers had used the interactive services. Most users were satisfied with these services, finding them easy to use and good with regard to speed.

Conversion to digital is thought likely to proceed at a slower pace from now on, partly because its growth had been driven by BSkyB switching its existing subscribers to digital, a task that is now largely complete. A survey by BMRB suggests that two-fifths of UK adults do not intend to get digital in the near future. If correct, this would hamper the government's plans to convert the nation to digital, as it has pledged not to turn off the analogue TV signal until 90 per cent of households have access to digital. To jump-start new growth in digital take-up, the government has announced plans to provide up to a thousand homes in several pilot areas with free conversion.

In the long term, it seems likely that most households will have access to digital, and with it the option to handle their finances by this means. However, in the medium term the picture is less clear and 't-finance' (television-finance) may remain a minority choice for some time to come.

There are three ways to access digital TV.

- **satellite** This is the most popular access method, accounting for over half of all digital viewers and potentially available to the majority of the population. The only UK provider at present is BSkyB. To access the service you need a digital set-top box (connected to your phone line if you want to use interactive services) and an appropriate satellite receiver – these are free if you subscribe to BSkyB. Services include Open, an interactive shopping channel. Financial firms available through Open in June 2001 were: Abbey National, HSBC and Woolwich, all offering e-banking (checking your balance, transferring money, paying bills) and information about other products; Cornhill Direct, offering life insurance, home insurance and pet insurance; and Norwich Union offering home and car insurance and individual savings accounts (ISAs). BSkyB does not currently offer Internet access, but may do so in future, which could open up the full range of web-finance services to users
- **terrestrial** Around 11 per cent of digital viewers use this method. As with satellite, you need a digital set-top box (connected to your phone line if you want to use interactive services), but instead of a satellite receiver you use your existing aerial. Not all areas can receive the digital signal. The only terrestrial service so far is ITV Digital (formerly called ONdigital). By adding an ITV Active subscription to the basic service you can access the Internet and also some financial services specific to ITV Active, including Abbey National, Cahoot, Barclays, Girobank and Egg.
- **cable** There are two main cable providers: NTL and Telewest. You can subscribe only if you live in an area served by the relevant company's cables. Around half the UK, mainly urban areas, can receive cable. At the time of writing, cable services offered only what is called 'walled garden' access to the Internet, whereby you can access only a limited selection of web sites; however NTL was planning full Internet access from 2001; and banking services were about to be added. Telewest included a number of money information sites, including Abbey National and Eagle Star insurance, and was about to add

e-banking. An advantage of cable is that you do not use your phone line to access the service.

Some digital TV and radio channels are free (called 'free-to-air' channels), and you can get these without paying any subscription. However, if you want to use interactive digital TV services, you'll need to sign up to one service or another. Costs vary, but are in the region of £7 to £12 per month. You may incur a connection fee of around £40, and you'll usually need to buy a keypad for around £30. Instead of a set-top box, you could buy an integrated digital TV, but bear in mind this could leave you using old technology for some time, while set-top box technology may well move on.

### Mobile phones

Wireless application protocol (WAP) phones let you access the Internet from your mobile phone. A number of financial services are available, including mobile banking and share information services. At present you have to dial up from your WAP phone each time you want to access the Net. However, the next generation of mobiles (General Packet Radio System – GPRS) will give you a permanent connection, removing the frustration of failed calls.

Despite the attraction of being able to bank on the move and check your share portfolio wherever you happen to be, WAP phones have so far not taken off. Fewer than one in 50 mobile users have access to the Net. Drawbacks include fiddly keypads, small screens and tricky navigation features. These may disappear in future, as mobile phones and palm-top computers look likely to converge into a single multifunction gadget.

WAP phones cost from around £40 to £270. Some banks are offering free WAP phones if you sign up for mobile banking. Call charges vary depending on the tariff you sign up for, but are usually in the range of 5p to 15p a minute.

## Finding your way around the Internet

Once you are hooked up to the Internet, how do you discover what financial providers are out there?

If you want to look up a particular company, you'll often hit lucky if you type in the company name preceded by 'www.' and suffixed with '.co.uk' or '.com'. If you are looking for a government or a regulator, the suffix will usually be '.gov.uk', and other official bodies or organisations that are not companies frequently use the ending '.org' or '.org.uk'.

If your ISP is a content provider, its home page will usually include a 'Money' or 'Finance' section with signposts to various relevant web sites. Another good site for this purpose is *www.find.co.uk*

The other main option is to use a search engine. Search engines constantly scour the Web using programs called 'spiders' and/or human editors to build up vast indexes based on words, titles and links. You can search the index to come up with sites that match the keywords you have supplied. Clicking on the link will take you to the web site you've found in the index. The table below lists some of the most widely used search engines.

## Commonly used search engines

| Name of search engine | Web site[1] |
| --- | --- |
| Alta Vista | *www.altavista.com* |
| Ask Jeeves | *www.askjeeves.com* |
| Direct Hit | *www.directhit.com* |
| Excite | *www.excite.com* |
| FAST Search | *www.alltheweb.com* |
| Google | *www.google.com* |
| HotBot | *www.hotbot.lycos.com* |
| LookSmart | *www.looksmart.com* |
| Lycos | *www.lycos.com* |
| MSN Search | *search.msn.com* |
| Netscape Search | *search.netscape.com* |
| Northern Light | *www.northernlight.com* |
| Open Directory | *dmoz.org* |
| Yahoo | *www.yahoo.com* |

1. For full address, prefix with 'http:'

You need to be careful with your choice of keywords, for example if you type in 'FSA' you're as likely to come up with the Football Supporters Association or Food Standards Agency as the Financial Services Authority. Sometimes you'll need to think laterally: if your first keyword doesn't come up with any results, try another related word. Often a search engine gives you the choice of searching the whole Web or just UK sites.

There are some standard symbols you can use when searching that can make your search more efficient (see the table below). The symbols will work with most major web sites. (You may also hear about 'Boolean operators'; these are mainly used by professionals, but are overkill for the average search and do not work in the same way with each search engine. The symbols in the table below should be adequate for most needs.)

**Useful symbols to improve your search**

| Symbol | What it does | Example |
|---|---|---|
| no symbol | Finds web pages that contain any of the words you list | **investment trust** will find pages containing 'investment' and/or 'trust' |
| + | Finds web pages that contain all the words you list, rather than just one or more of them | **investment+trust** will find pages containing 'investment' and 'trust' |
| – | Finds web pages with the first word you list but not the second | **investment-ISA** will find pages containing 'investment' but not those that also contain 'ISA' |
| " " | Finds web pages with the exact phrase you have put in quotes | **"investment trust"** will find pages containing the phrase 'investment trust' |
| Combined symbols | Refines your search | **"investment trust"-ISA** will find pages containing the phrase 'investment trust' but not those also containing 'ISA' |

# Banking online

**5**

A current account is a near-essential tool of day-to-day money management. Being able to run your account from home – or indeed anywhere else in the world – could prove very convenient. Many traditional banks are now offering Internet banking to customers as an option with their normal banking products, so you can choose to go to a branch, phone up or go online – this is sometimes called a 'bricks-and-clicks' service. There are also a few Internet-only banks offering accounts designed to be operated only or mainly online, including Cahoot, First-e, Intelligent Finance and Smile. (Egg is another well-known Internet-only bank, but at the time of writing it does not offer a current account.)

There are two aspects to consider when choosing any Internet product: the features of the product itself and the features of the Internet service.

## Current accounts – the product

Current accounts come in three basic forms:

- **full accounts offering a comprehensive range of services** – for example cheque book, cash card, debit card, standing orders, direct debits and overdrafts
- **full accounts offering most services but no overdraft**
- **basic banking accounts** offering a limited range of services, for example cash card, debit card (usually Solo or Electron), direct debits and standing orders. A few also offer a cheque book. In general, these accounts are aimed at those who have not previously used a bank and to help people manage their money without the risk of going into debt.

Within each group, the range of facilities offered by different accounts tends to be fairly homogeneous. The main differences are quality of service, the interest rate offered on credit balances and the charges if you go overdrawn. The tables on pages 61 and 62 compare the interest rates offered in June 2001 by the main current accounts available over the Internet in each of the three main groups. Rates change over time, as general interest rates in the economy rise and fall and as banks compete with each other for your custom, so you need to check the rates current at the time you are shopping around.

A point to note is that some accounts – marked with '†' in the tables – offer much higher rates than others, and these tend to be the Internet-only banks. However, high interest rates are important only if on average you have a fairly high current account balance. If you make a habit of shifting excess funds into a savings account, a high rate on your current account will earn you only a few pounds extra each year. Internet accounts make it particularly easy to transfer funds between current and savings accounts. Sweeper accounts (see overleaf) do this automatically.

*Which?* Magazine regularly surveys current accounts, asking its readers how satisfied they are with their bank. Internet-only banks do not as yet have enough *Which?*-reading customers to appear in the rankings. However, among the traditional banks that now offer an Internet service, the following were rated as best buys by *Which?* in January 2001 and also scored highly on satisfaction among *Which?* readers:

- **if you're always in credit (in other words don't run up an overdraft)**: First Direct, Nationwide
- **if you tend to have a small arranged overdraft (£100 for one week per quarter)**: Alliance & Leicester, First Direct, HSBC, Nationwide, Royal Bank of Scotland
- **if you tend to have a larger arranged overdraft (£500 for two weeks a month)**: Alliance & Leicester, First Direct, HSBC, Nationwide.

## Sweeper accounts

A handful of financial providers offer sweeper accounts that combine your current account and a savings account with the same provider. Any amount above a prearranged current account balance is automatically transferred into a savings account, where it earns higher interest. Examples include Abbey National, Barclays (Platinum Banking), First Direct, HSBC, Halifax (Current Account), Intelligent Finance (Current Account), NatWest and Royal Bank of Scotland.

## Combined accounts

Another variation is the combined account. With a combined account, your current account can be combined with savings accounts, credit cards, loans and a mortgage from the same provider. Interest is worked out on the combined balance of all the accounts.

If you have a mortgage, the net result is that you pay interest on the combined negative balance. Money paid into your current or savings accounts reduces the outstanding balance and so the interest due. By saving you interest payments, in effect, your current account and savings are earning the mortgage rate and, moreover, the interest 'earned' is tax free.

If you don't have a mortgage or any other borrowings, interest is earned on your combined current and savings account balances (which may take you into a higher rate interest tier).

In general these combined accounts are a good deal provided you have a mortgage and don't mind having all your eggs in one basket. If you don't have a mortgage, the advantage of a combined account is much less, and you might do better to shop around for separate products.

Financial providers offering combined accounts available by Internet include Intelligent Finance, Virgin (One) and Woolwich (Open Plan).

# Interest rates offered on full Internet current accounts

| Bank | Account | Interest rate on £500 balance (%) |
|---|---|---|
| Abbey National | Bank Account | 0.1 |
| Alliance & Leicester | Alliance | 0.25 |
| | Alliance Premier | 0.25 |
| Bank of Scotland | Chequeplus | 0.1 |
| | Direct Current Account | 0.1 |
| Barclays | Bank account | 0.1 |
| | Platinum Banking | 0.1 |
| | Additions | 0.1 |
| †Cahoot | Current Account with cheque book | 5.84 |
| | Current Account – without chequebook | 6.03 |
| Citibank | Current Account | 0.1 |
| Co-operative | Current Account | none |
| First Direct | Bank account | 1 |
| | Cheque Account | 0.1 |
| HSBC | Bank Account | 0.1 |
| | Premier Bank Account | 0.1 |
| †Halifax | Current Account | 4.0 |
| †Intelligent Finance | Current Account | 4.41 |
| Lloyds-TSB | Classic | 0.1 |
| | Select | 0.1 |
| | Gold Service | 0.1 |
| | Platinum Current | 0.1 |
| Nationwide | Flexaccount | 1.0 |
| NatWest | Current | none |
| | Current Plus | 0.1 |
| | Advantage Gold | 0.25 |
| | Advantage Premier | 0.5 |
| Norwich and | Netmaster Gold | 0.35 |
| Peterborough | Gold Current | 0.35 |
| Royal Bank of Scotland | IPCA | 0.1 |
| | Royalties | 0.2 |
| | Royalties Gold | 0.5 |
| †Smile | Current Account | 4.0 |
| †Virgin | One | 3.25 |
| Woolwich | Open Plan | 1.25 |

*Source*: *Moneyfacts*, June 2001 and supplementary research.
†Accounts offering the highest rates.

## Interest rates offered on full Internet current accounts without overdrafts

| Bank | Account | Interest rate on £500 balance (%) |
| --- | --- | --- |
| Bank of Scotland | Money Market Cheque | 0.25 |
| Barclays | Prime Account | n/a |
| †First-e | Current Account | 4.25 |

*Source*: *Moneyfacts*, June 2001.

## Interest rates offered on basic Internet current accounts

| Bank | Account | Interest rate on £500 balance (%) |
| --- | --- | --- |
| Abbey National | Instant Plus | 0.1 |
| Alliance & Leicester | Basic Banking Account | 0.25 |
| Bank of Scotland | Easycash | none |
| Co-operative Bank | Cashminder | none |
| †First-e | Current Account | 4.25 |
| HSBC | Basic Banking | none |
| Halifax | Cardcash | none |
| †Intelligent Finance | Current Account (Basic) | 4.41 |
| Nationwide | Flexaccount (Basic) | 1.0 |
| NatWest | Step | 0.1 |
| Royal Bank of Scotland | Key | 0.1 |

*Source*: *Moneyfacts*, June 2001

## Current accounts – the Internet service

The basic online service is broadly similar for all current accounts and includes the following features.

### Access

Virtually all online banking services are available 24 hours, every day of the year. However, all services reserve the right to be down from time to time, for example to allow for maintenance. And, although you can give instructions to your bank around the clock, they might not be carried out until the next working day.

In general, you will need a computer with a Pentium processor. You'll usually need a fairly recent version of whichever browser you're using.

## *Paying money in and getting cash out*

Many Internet banking services are options with ordinary bank accounts, so you have all the bricks-and-mortar banking facilities too. This means you can pay in cash and cheques at a branch if you want to, as well as relying on automated credits. You can withdraw cash at branches or cash machines and usually have a cheque book that can be used as an alternative to automated transfers.

With Internet-only banks, paying-in arrangements vary. For example, Smile has arranged for post offices to accept cash and cheque deposits. First-e does not accept cash at all, but you can post cheques. To withdraw cash from an Internet bank, you use cash machines, and you can usually have a cheque book to use as an alternative to automated transfers.

## *Logging in*

With most Internet banking services, the web address takes you to a home page. A link from there takes you direct to the log-in page, where you will typically be asked to type in an identification code (also called a 'registration code' or 'security code') and password ('passcode').

If you have a joint account with another person, you'll each have your own code and password. You should not tell each other your code or password.

| Welcome to E-Z BANK. |
| --- |
| Please type in your ID and password |
| ID    ******* |
| Password    ********* |
| Log in ○     Help ○ |

## Viewing your account(s)

In most cases, the screen you will see directly after logging in is a summary of your account and any other products offered by the same provider that are covered by the online service; for example, you might be operating a current account and one or more savings accounts online. Some services also let you include, say, credit-card accounts, loans, your mortgage, individual savings accounts (ISAs), unit trusts and stakeholder pensions.

The summary shows the name of the account, its number and the balance. Some services distinguish between the balance in the account and the cleared balance. A cleared balance excludes items that have been paid but where the administration required to transfer money from another account has not been completed and so could be stopped (if, say, a cheque bounced). The cleared balance shows the amount that is actually in your account and available for use straight away.

---

E-Z BANK

### View your accounts

| Account name | Account number | Balance | Available balance |
|---|---|---|---|
| E-Z Current | xx106542893 | £342.07 | £302.07 |
| E-Z savings | xz5249-66 | £758.32 | £758.32 |
| E-Z mini cash ISA | xz8880-01 | £3,000.00 | £3,000.00 |

Please select an account to view

Submit ○          Clear ○

---

Selecting one of the accounts in the summary takes you to a more detailed screen where you can view your recent transactions. How far back you can go varies from one service to another – for example, you might be able to see the last 40 or 99 transactions or go back 90 days or as far as two years.

Often you can opt to see particular types of transaction only – for example, just cash machine withdrawals or cheques or standing orders.

E-Z BANK

Account xx106542893   Date 27/06/01

Current balance £342.07   Available balance £302.07

| Date | Description | Amount | Balance | ▲ |
|------|-------------|--------|---------|---|
| 27/06/01 | Credit | £40.00 | £342.07 | |
| 22/06/01 | DD | £46.66 | £302.07 | |
| 21/06/01 | ATM | £100.00 | £348.73 | |
| 20/06/01 | DD | £300.00 | £448.73 | |
| 20/06/01 | DD | £257.63 | £748.73 | |
| 20/06/01 | ATM | £50.00 | £1,006.36 | |
| 13/06/01 | ATM | £100.00 | £1,056.36 | |
| 08/06/01 | Cheque | £60.00 | £1,156.36 | |
| 06/06/01 | ATM | £100.00 | £1,216.36 | |
| 04/06/01 | DD | £32.00 | £1,316.36 | ▼ |

View the last 90 transactions

View only: ATM withdrawals ○ Cheques ○ Standing orders ○ Direct debits ○

## *Transfers between accounts and 'third-party payments'*

You can usually transfer money between your current account and other accounts you have with the same provider online. In order to do this, you will sometimes need to set up a direct debit from your current account, which is then used as the channel for transfers in either direction.

Most services also let you transfer to and from any other UK account, allowing you to make payments to any person or firm that has an account (called 'third-party payments'). A few services – for example, Citibank – let you shift money to or from certain accounts held outside the UK.

You'll need the sort code of the bank or building society and the account number and name. Typically, you set up a profile for the person or firm you want to pay, and this is stored on the system. Whenever you want to pay that person or firm, you simply call up the details and specify the amount to be paid.

Transfers can be set up as one-off payments or as regular payments. You can alter or cancel them at any time.

Generally, transfers are immediate between accounts held with the same provider, or take about four working days in other cases. Some services let you set up transfers in advance – even up to three years in advance – in which case you may be able to choose whether to specify the date the payment leaves your account or the date it arrives.

---

E-Z BANK

## Setting up a payment

| | |
|---|---|
| From your account | xx106542893 |
| Name of recipient | MISS N LONG |
| Their account number | 54678921 |
| Their sort code | 99 55 01 |
| Their reference | |
| Name you have given to this recipient/payment | TASHA |

Submit ○          Clear ○

---

## *Paying bills*

Essentially, paying a bill is the same as transferring money from your account to another, in this case the account of the firm that is billing you. With many services, you can easily add a new bill to your account using an online procedure. With a few services, you have to give your bank the details of the new payee and let it set up the arrangement; you can then use it online in the normal way.

Some services include a menu of the most common payees – for example local authorities (for council tax), water companies, gas suppliers and so on. This could be handy, saving you the trouble of searching for the firm's sort code and account number, but to be on the safe side it's a good idea to check the details provided online against the payment instructions on a recent bill. If the firm you want to pay is not on a menu, you may be able to set up the payment online yourself, or you might need to phone your bank to do this.

Bills can be set up as one-off or ad hoc payments, or as regular payments. Regular payments can be set up as standing orders or direct debits.

As with other transfers, some services let you set up bill payments in advance – even up to two years in advance – in which case you may be able to choose whether to specify the date the money leaves your account or the date it arrives with the payee.

---

E-Z BANK

**Making a payment**

| | |
|---|---|
| From your account | xx106542893 |
| Available balance | £302.07 |
| Name you have given to this recipient/bill | GAS |
| Amount | £58.23 |

Allow four working days for payments to arrive

Submit ○     Clear ○

---

## Standing orders and direct debits

Most services let you set up standing orders yourself while you are online. A few require you to give your bank the details so that it can set up the arrangement for you. You can view, alter and cancel standing orders online. If you cancel an order, the details usually remain recorded in the system, so that you can easily reactivate the order if you want to.

You cannot set up direct debits online. Direct debits are your permission to your bank to let someone else draw payments from your account, so they are set up by your bank and the firm to whom payment is to be made. However, you can view and cancel direct debits online.

---

E-Z BANK

## Setting up a standing order

| | |
|---|---|
| Name you have given to this recipient/payment | COUNCIL TAX |
| To be paid from your account | xx106542893 |
| Name of recipient | SOMERSHIRE DISTRICT COUNCIL |
| Their account number | 98765432 |
| Their sort code | 88  22  18 |
| Their reference | W1000340056 |
| Amount | £103.00 |

**Type of standing order**

Until further notice ○ Paid between set dates ○ Set number of transactions ○

| | |
|---|---|
| Start date | 02  04  01 |
| Frequency | MONTHLY |

Allow four working days for payment to arrive

Amend ○          Cancel ○

---

## *Other services*

The range of other facilities offered online may include being able to request an overdraft or loan, ordering new PINs for cash cards and credit cards, ordering a cheque book and so on.

Usually there will be a secure messaging facility. You should never include account information in ordinary emails because they are not a secure form of communication. The secure messaging facility uses encryption, which makes it very unlikely that someone could intercept and read the contents, and so is a safe way for you and your bank to discuss your account.

## *Downloading into your money-management software*

Many online banking services are compatible with Microsoft Money, Intuit Quicken and sometimes spread-sheets, such as Microsoft Excel, so you can download your account statements directly into your money-management software.

## Bricks-and-mortar contact details

Chapter 2 discussed the importance of noting down a bricks-and-mortar address and phone number before doing business with a firm online. Although you may feel confident that a household-name bank or building society is not a fly-by-night organisation, it can still be very inconvenient if you do not have a phone number or address to hand when you need to get in touch.

If you are using the Internet option with an account you opened at a bricks-and-mortar branch, the contact details might seem unimportant as you always have the option of contacting your branch. But increasingly, even with these banking services, you can open a new account online without ever developing a relationship with a branch, so it is important that you have a telephone number and an address for written enquiries.

All the banks and building societies looked at provided an email link, but a survey carried out in 2000 suggests this can be a frustratingly slow way to get a response. IT consultancy Vanson Bourne sent an email to 30 online banks posing as a prospective customer seeking information; 20 banks failed to reply within a day, and a third did not reply at all. Of those that did reply, nearly half gave an incomplete or irrelevant answer. The response was even worse when a second, more complicated query was submitted. The big high-street banks tended to be the worst, and Internet banks did only moderately well in the survey.

It is hard to be confident that banks are tackling this problem. A separate survey by MORI found that the banks were quite pleased with their perceived response times: half of those surveyed believed they responded to emails within 7 hours, and two-thirds within 14 hours.

Most of the online banking sites covered from page 75 onwards operate a phone-based helpdesk, nearly always on a local-rate line. However, you might have to trawl through a user guide or frequently asked questions (FAQ) page to find the number. Other places to find contact details included the 'Help' or 'Important legal information' options, or the very small print at the bottom of the home page. Top marks went to First Direct, Norwich and Peterborough's Netmaster Gold, and Smile and Virgin, which all had a prominent 'Contact us' or similar links that took you straight to a summary of telephone numbers and addresses to write to.

Frustratingly, a few sites (such as First-e and Cahoot) used 'Contact us' to open an email screen with no bricks-and-mortar address in sight.

## Privacy

A privacy policy or statement about how the bank or building society would use your information could not be found on the sites of six of the banking services looked at – Bank of Scotland, Barclays, Co-operative, Nationwide, Norwich and Peterborough, and Virgin. In other cases, the policy was often buried in the terms and conditions, under legal information, and in one case somewhat obscurely under 'Contact us'. Four sites stood out as having very prominent privacy policies: Cahoot, Citibank, First-e and HSBC.

In general, the policies simply echo the requirements of the Data Protection Act (see Chapter 2). A good policy also tells you, for example, whether the web site uses 'cookies' and how to get in touch if you don't want to receive product information.

## Security and your liability if things go wrong

Nearly all the banking services reviewed had clear information about security, often with a prominent link from the home page.

As standard, banking services use a high level of encryption (128-bit secure socket layer – see Chapter 2). You are given some form of registration number and a password, which you must use to access the account. Usually, failure on, say, three attempts to enter these correctly results in your account being locked. Most sites 'time out' if you are online but have not interacted with the site for a while – time-out periods vary from around five to ten minutes. Different banks use a variety of other security features. For example, First-e issues you with transaction authorisation numbers (TANs). Each time you carry out a transaction you provide one of the TANs as a sort of signature.

There are a variety of steps you can take to make your banking sessions more secure – see the box pn page 73.

When it comes to online banking, the major concern of most people is that someone will fraudulently access their account and take money from it. Good security should make this unlikely; however if the chips were down you would want to know who would bear the loss:

- Halifax and Intelligent Finance (a division of the Halifax) are unique in offering a no-strings guarantee that you will not bear any loss if you are a victim of fraud. Some others protect you provided you have followed the security steps in the terms and conditions (see overleaf)
- some services – including Citibank, Norwich and Peterborough (Netmaster Gold), Smile and Woolwich – limit your loss to a maximum of £50 up to the time you inform them of a problem and nothing thereafter

(provided you have not been grossly negligent or involved in the fraud)
- others – such as Alliance & Leicester, Bank of Scotland, First-e, NatWest and Virgin – leave you to bear the full amount of any loss up to the time you inform them of the problem.

Any protection offered by the bank is usually conditional upon your observing the security requirements it imposes on you (and provided you have not been grossly negligent or involved in the fraud). You need to read the security requirements carefully as they vary from bank to bank. For example, most services sensibly forbid you to write down your security codes in any way that can be readily recognised, but a few – including Cahoot, Smile and Woolwich – forbid you to write down your codes at all. While memorising your codes is certainly the best policy, this can be difficult if you are required to remember several sets of codes for a number of different products. Norwich and Peterborough can leave you liable for losses if you do not have up-to-date anti-virus software on your computer, or have accessed the service from a computer that is not your own. Anti-virus software is a good idea, but it can be an onerous task to check that it is always up to date – Halifax takes a more reasonable approach by supplying customers with free anti-virus software. One of Alliance & Leicester's conditions is that you change your 'passphrase' at least every 90 days.

You'll find the security requirements in the terms and conditions, which themselves are not always easy to locate on the web site, though you should be sent a copy once you sign up for a service. If they are not readily visible, try looking under 'Legal information' or on the page where you register for the service or log in. Annoyingly, terms and conditions sometimes pop up in a separate window with no print button. You can print off a permanent record by right-clicking your mouse and selecting 'Print' from the menu that appears. Alternatively, right-click and choose 'Select All', right-click again and choose 'Copy', then past the text into your word-processing software, from which you can print.

# Tips on banking safely online

- make sure that nobody else can overlook you while you are using the service. If you are in a public place, beware of being in view of security cameras

- if possible, use a computer that you do not share (some banking services require this)

- if you take a break during a session (for example to visit the bathroom or get a cup of coffee), do not leave the computer connected to the service. Log off before leaving the machine and then log on again on your return

- at the end of your session, log off. If you don't log off, someone else could access your accounts. Also, logging off helps to clear sensitive information from the computer

- if you share a computer (for example, it is at work, in a cybercafé or library), empty the cache on your browser after the session – again, this will ensure that sensitive information is not retained on the computer. To find out how to do this, consult the 'Help' file on your browser

- destroy any paperwork notifying security codes

- if possible memorise your codes. If you must write them down, disguise them and do not keep them with other banking materials, such as a cash card. Some services prohibit you from writing down your codes

- choose a password that is easy for you to remember but is not obvious to anyone else. Avoid birth dates, consecutive numbers and repeated numbers. A combination of numbers and letters is more secure than just numbers or just letters

- do not tell your security codes to anyone, even employees of the bank or building society. Some services might ask you for one or two digits or letters, but you should never be asked for the full code

- if you suspect someone else knows your codes, change them at once and tell the bank or building society immediately

- for a copy of the Banking Code and a useful guide to online banking, visit the web site of the British Bankers Association at *www.bba.org.uk*.

## The Banking Code of Practice

All the major UK banks and building societies subscribe to the Banking Code of Practice. First-e, which is a Dublin-based French bank, also subscribes to the code.

The code, which is voluntary, sets out minimum standards of good practice in banks' and building societies' dealings with their customers and prospective customers. It covers, for example, requirements to provide you with information to help you choose accounts and to keep you up-to-date with charges and changes in interest rates, your right to a 14-day cooling-off period, during which you without loss can change your mind about opening an account (other than a fixed rate account), and the limiting of your loss to a maximum of £50 if someone uses your plastic card(s) without authority.

## Complaints and compensation

The banking code also requires subscribers to have in place a formal complaints procedure and access to an independent dispute-resolution service. UK banks are covered by the Financial Ombudsman Service (FOS),* which from November 2001 replaces the earlier Banking Ombudsman and Building Society Ombudsman schemes. The FOS has the power to order banks and building societies to pay redress up to £100,000.

UK banks are also covered by the Financial Services Compensation Scheme,* which, from November 2001, can pay out 100 per cent of the first £2,000 you have deposited and 90 per cent of the next £33,000 (a maximum of £31,700 in total) if you lose money due to the failure of a bank or building society.

Under the rules of the FOS, First-e is not currently able to join and, and as a result has established its own independent dispute-resolution scheme available to members. The scheme is able to make awards up to £250,000, which are binding on First-e but not on you. First-e is also outside the scope of the Financial Services Compensation Scheme but is covered by an equivalent French scheme that provides protection up to €70,000 (worth just under £42,000 in June 2001).

## Summary of online services

Below is the low-down on 20 of the main e-banking services currently available. To some extent, how each person perceives a service is subjective – for example, the layout and navigation that seems clear to one person may not find favour with another, and extras valuable to one person may not be of use to someone else. Therefore, not all services have been ranked here. However, where a service strikes us as particularly good, it has been given a ✓ symbol and you might want to check it out. A few services have been marked with ✕, a warning that you could suffer unlimited losses in the event of fraudulent use of your account.

Bear in mind that, as well as getting along with the online service itself, you must make sure the provider offers the type of current account that suits you (see page 58).

## Abbey National
## www.abbeynational.co.uk

TYPE OF SERVICE: Option available with its traditional bank accounts.

BASICS: As set out on pages 62–9. Can be used with a current account, some savings accounts, mini cash ISAs. Account must be linked to an Abbey National Multifunction card, Electron card or Abbeylink card. Online statements let you view the last 40 transactions.

SUPPORT: Local-rate helpline open Monday to Saturday, 7am to 11pm.

DOWNLOAD TO MONEY-MANAGEMENT SOFTWARE: Not at present.

CONTACT DETAILS: 'Contact us' on the home page links to a variety of phone numbers and an address for complaints.

PRIVACY: No readily accessible outline of this bank's privacy policy. When the site was checked out, the User Guide, which you can view online (right-click your mouse to print it out) contained a heading 'Using your information' but – presumably in error – there were no details.

SECURITY AND LIABILITY: You can link to a very brief security statement from the log-in screen and find a few more details in the terms and conditions, which is part of the 'How to register' screen. Security information can be printed easily.

Abbey National guarantees to cover any losses from e-banking fraud, provided you have taken the necessary steps to safe-guard your passcode and registration number. The safeguards are laid out in the terms and conditions and are all reasonable: for example, don't tell anyone your passcode or registration number, don't let anyone else use them, never write them down without disguising them, and so on.

OTHER: Speed of downloading pages was good. Efficient colour-coded navigation. Abbey National says it is developing a service for the partially sighted. It also offers banking by mobile phone and interactive digital TV.

## Alliance & Leicester
## www.alliance-leicester.co.uk

> ✗ – you are unacceptably exposed in the event of fraud.

TYPE OF SERVICE: Option available with traditional bank accounts.

BASICS: As set out on pages 62–9. Can be used with current accounts and various savings accounts. Statements let you view the last 46 working days.

SUPPORT: Helpline.

DOWNLOAD TO MONEY-MANAGEMENT SOFTWARE: Not at present.

CONTACT DETAILS: Easy to find under 'About us'.

PRIVACY: In the terms and conditions. You are deemed to have agreed to having your data passed on to other companies in the group and will need to write in if you don't want to receive information about their products.

SECURITY AND LIABILITY: No details about security measures, other than the security codes and phrases you use. Some of the conditions are quite onerous: for example, you must agree to use an up-to-date virus-scanning program on material downloaded from the service, and, if you are to escape liability for losses due to fraud, you must inter alia change your passphrase at least every 90 days. The terms and conditions state: 'The bank shall not be liable for any loss or damage you may incur in the bank acting upon any instructions received using the security information'. This leaves you to carry any loss if your account is used fraudulently.

OTHER: Speed of downloading pages is good, navigation reasonable. Site includes a range of useful calculators – for example to work out mortgage repayments and help you plan your budget.

## Bank of Scotland
## www.bankofscotland.co.uk

> ✕ – you are unacceptably exposed in the event of fraud.

TYPE OF SERVICE: Option available with traditional bank accounts.

BASICS: As outlined on pages 62–9. Statements let you view last 45 working days. You can arrange payments up to 30 days in advance.

SUPPORT: Local-rate helpline, 24 hours a day, 363 days a year.

DOWNLOAD TO MONEY-MANAGEMENT SOFTWARE: Microsoft Money and Intuit Quicken.

CONTACT DETAILS: Follow 'Get in touch' from the home page. At the next screen, 'General enquiry' just opens email, but 'Offices and divisions' gives you bricks-and-mortar addresses and phone numbers.

PRIVACY: No privacy policy found.

SECURITY AND LIABILITY: Prominent security policy including comprehensive guidance on the precautions you should take. You also need to read the terms and conditions – very small print on the application form. You are required to change your passwords at least every 12 months. In case of fraudulent use of your account, you are liable for any loss – however large – up to the time you notify the bank.

OTHER: Speed fairly slow at the time of checking.

## Barclays bank
## www.ibank.barclays.co.uk

TYPE OF SERVICE: Option available with traditional bank accounts.

BASICS: As outlined on pages 62–9. You can view the last six weeks' transactions.

SUPPORT: Local-rate helpline, Monday to Friday 7am to 11pm,

Saturday and Sunday 9am to 5pm.

DOWNLOAD TO MONEY-MANAGEMENT SOFTWARE: Microsoft Money and spreadsheets (including Microsoft Excel).

CONTACT DETAILS: 'Feedback' on the home page just gives you the option to email the company, and, try as we might, we failed to find any route to a bricks-and-mortar address or phone number.

PRIVACY: No privacy policy found.

SECURITY AND LIABILITY: Easy-to-find security policy, supplemented by further information under 'Questions you're asking'. Unable to find any terms and conditions or similar information regarding liability.

OTHER: You can customise the service to some extent – for example choosing the layout of statements. Site includes some calculators – for example to work out loan repayments and see whether you can cut your utility bills.

---

## Cahoot
### www.cahoot.com

TYPE OF SERVICE : Abbey National's dedicated Internet bank.

BASICS: As outlined on pages 62–9. View the last 12 months' statements. Arrange payments up to a year in advance. Cahoot's current account offers a free £250 overdraft limit and three options for larger overdrafts with different charges tailored to suit different types of borrower.

SUPPORT: Local-rate helpline.

DOWNLOAD TO MONEY-MANAGEMENT SOFTWARE: Not at present.

CONTACT DETAILS: The only address to be found was the registered office in small print at the foot of the home page. 'Contact us' simply opens up email.

PRIVACY: Prominent policy on home page.

SECURITY AND LIABILITY: Security section prominently listed on the home page. Terms and conditions detail liability. Provided you keep to the security requirements (which are all reasonable), you are not liable for any loss due to unauthorised use of your account.

OTHER: Layout of web site is admirably clear. The FAQ section is a bit tedious to use, as you have to click on each question in turn to reveal the answer, instead of being able to scroll down a continuous list. In support of this bank's fun image, the site includes a couple of games. Cahoot also offers WAP phone banking and at the time of writing offered users a free WAP phone. It intends to offer interactive digital TV banking from early 2002.

## Citibank
### www.citibank.com/uk

TYPE OF SERVICE: Complements its existing postal and phone banking services.

BASICS: As outlined on pages 62–9. View the last 99 transactions over the last 90 days. Option to print off a summary of your transactions at the end of each session. As well as UK transfers, you can move money to and from Citibank accounts in Belgium, France, Germany, Greece and Luxembourg, and view the exchange rate before completing the transaction. To qualify for a Citibank account, you must earn at least £20,000 a year and either have your salary paid directly into the account or deposit at least £2,000.

SUPPORT: Free helpline.

DOWNLOAD TO MONEY-MANAGEMENT SOFTWARE: Microsoft Money, Intuit Quicken and Microsoft Excel spreadsheets.

CONTACT DETAILS: Follow 'Help desk' and then 'Customer services', where you'll find a comprehensive list of phone numbers and branch addresses.

PRIVACY: Prominent link from home page; clear and comprehensive policy. A nice touch is that Citibank asserts it will contact you at least once a year to tell you how you can remove your name from marketing lists, in addition to your right at any time to instruct the bank on this.

SECURITY AND LIABILITY: Prominent link to security statement from home page. Your maximum liability is £50 up to the time you notify Citibank, and nothing thereafter.

OTHER: Magazine-type feel to the site, which includes news and a range of other online financial services such as share information. To some extent you can personalise the site by specifying your own home page and choosing shortcuts. Step-by-step guide and letters you need to transfer your account to Citibank.

## Co-operative
### www.co-operativebank.co.uk

TYPE OF SERVICE: Option available with traditional bank accounts.

BASICS: As outlined on pages 62–9. View current and savings accounts, loans and credit-card information. View the last six months' statements. To set up bill payments and fund transfers you first need to phone the bank; once they are set up, you operate them online. When maintenance is necessary, it usually takes place between 3 and 3.30am from Monday to Saturday, or midnight to 6am on Sunday.

SUPPORT: Local-rate line for banking instructions. National-rate technical helpline, 8am to 10pm, 7 days a week.

DOWNLOAD TO MONEY-MANAGEMENT SOFTWARE: Not at present.

CONTACT DETAILS: Easily found under 'About the bank'.

PRIVACY: No privacy policy found.

SECURITY AND LIABILITY: Security statement easily found and supplemented by information in the 'Question and answer' section. Terms and conditions require that you never write down your security codes. You are liable for up to £50 of any loss up to the time you notify the bank there is a problem, and nothing thereafter.

OTHER: Co-operative operates in accordance with an ethical policy, setting out with whom it will and will not do business.

## First Direct
### www.firstdirect.com

TYPE OF SERVICE: Complements existing phone-banking service.

BASICS: As outlined on pages 62–9. Covers current and savings accounts and mini cash ISAs.

SUPPORT: Local-rate helpline, 7am to midnight, 365 days a year. Local-rate technical support, 4pm to midnight on weekdays and 8am to midnight at weekends.

DOWNLOAD TO MONEY-MANAGEMENT SOFTWARE: Microsoft Money, Intuit Quicken, Microsoft Excel spreadsheets and other software.

CONTACT DETAILS: Easily found under 'Contact us'.

PRIVACY: Policy tucked away in the terms and conditions, which you'll find on the application form (right-click your mouse to print). You'll need to tell the bank if you don't want your details used for marketing purposes.

SECURITY AND LIABILITY: Details about security included in the outline of the service. Provided you observe the security conditions (which are reasonable), you are not liable for any losses due to fraudulent use of your account.

OTHER: First Direct also offers WAP phone banking and PC banking (computer banking that uses bank software installed on your home computer). At the time of writing, it was also offering customers £100 discount when buying a Dell PC.

## First-e
## www.first-e.co.uk

---

| ✗ – you are unacceptably exposed in the event of fraud. |
| --- |

TYPE OF SERVICE: Internet-only bank.

BASICS: As outlined on pages 62–9. Service covers current and savings accounts. You cannot pay cash into an account. You can make payments to and receive transfers from non-UK bank accounts but there will be a charge (£10 or £20). There is no charge for UK-only transfers. Because First-e is an offshore bank, it pays interest to UK residents gross (without any tax deducted). If you are a taxpayer, you must declare this interest to the Inland Revenue and pay the tax due. However, under the self-assessment tax system, there can be a substantial delay (up to 20 months) between earning the interest and paying the tax. In the meantime, you earn interest on the unpaid tax, giving you a bit of a bonus – but the amount will be small unless you have very large sums in your account.

SUPPORT: A call centre is available, but the bank discourages you from using it. If you make a transaction by phone rather than Internet, there is a £5 charge.

DOWNLOAD TO MONEY-MANAGEMENT SOFTWARE: Not at present.

CONTACT DETAILS: 'Contact us' buttons lead to the email service. Under 'Complaints process' you'll find an address for written complaints. No telephone numbers are given on the site, but a call-centre number for users is supplied when you sign up.

PRIVACY: Easily accessed from the home page and very comprehensive. Further information included in the 'Help' section.

Security and liability: Easily accessed from 'About us' menu on the home page. Comprehensive statement and useful security tips. As well as an identity code and password, First-e sends you by secure email Transaction Authorisation Numbers (TANs) which are effectively digital signatures – you use one TAN to authorise each transaction. The terms and conditions would not win any plain English awards, and it is hard to pin down liability in the event of unauthorised use of your account. If misuse occurs through fraudulent use of your debit card, your loss is limited to £100 until the bank is notified, and nothing thereafter, provided you've observed the terms and conditions. Fraud not related to debit cards seems to be covered by the statement: 'The bank will not be liable for any loss of, or any failure to ensure investments or for the quality, quantity, condition or delivery thereof or the correctness, validity, sufficiency or genuineness of any of the documents relating thereto'. In other words, you could lose an unlimited amount.

Other: The FAQ section is a bit fiddly, with two tiers of menu before you get to the answers. A nice touch is that you can download the Internet banking demonstration to run offline in your own time. First-e is based in Dublin but run by a French bank (Banque d'Escompte) and regulated by the French authorities. Being ineligible for the Financial Ombudsman Scheme, the bank has set up its own independent dispute resolution scheme. The relevant compensation scheme offers slightly more protection than the equivalent UK scheme. First-e also offers WAP phone banking.

## Halifax
**www.halifax-online.co.uk**

Type of service: Option available with traditional bank accounts.

Basics: As outlined on pages 62–9. Service covers current and savings accounts. You can also include some credit-card accounts. View the last 60 account transactions.

Support: Local rate, 24 hours a day, 7 days a week.

Download to money-management software: Not at present.

Contact details: 'Contact us' leads only to an email link.

Privacy: Under 'Contact us', or follow the link to the Halifax corporate site to view the 'Privacy and security' policy there. Alternatively, click on the link from FAQ.

Security and liability: The security policy is discussed in the FAQ section, and you are invited to phone the support line for more information. Halifax guarantees that you will not be liable for any loss if you are the victim of fraud.

Other: Once you've signed up, Halifax offers free anti-virus software. Note that the Halifax service cannot be used with Apple Mac computers, only PCs. Halifax also offers mobile phone banking.

## HSBC
**www.hsbc.co.uk**

Type of service: Option available with traditional bank accounts.

Basics: As outlined on pages 62–9. Covers your current and savings accounts, credit card, private banking, loan accounts, mortgages and stakeholder pensions. View the last 90 transactions from the last 65 days. You can set up transfers and bill payments up to a year in advance.

Support: Local-rate helpline, Monday to Saturday 8am to 10pm, Sunday 10am to 8pm.

Download to money-management software: Microsoft Money, Intuit Quicken and spreadsheets.

Contact details: 'Useful contacts' leads to a range of phone numbers. 'Find a branch' lets you look up your local bricks-and-mortar bank.

Privacy: Link to the privacy policy from home page and information also given in the terms and conditions. Both can be printed off easily.

Security and liability: The security arrangements are described in the 'User guide'. However, you'll need to right-click your mouse to print this off – cumbersome, especially since the User Guide forms part of the terms and conditions. You are not liable for any loss due to fraudulent use of your account, provided you observe the security requirements set out in the terms and conditions – these are pretty standard and reasonable. Note that you agree to check your transactions and statements carefully.

Other: HSBC also offers interactive digital TV banking.

## Intelligent Finance
## www.if.com

TYPE OF SERVICE: Halifax's dedicated Internet (and phone) bank.

BASICS: As outlined on pages 62–9. Covers current and savings accounts, mortgage accounts, personal loan accounts and credit-card accounts. This is a 'combined service' (see page 60) where the interest you pay or receive depends on the combined total of the balances in all the accounts. Provided you are a borrower, this means some or all of the funds in your current and/or savings account in effect 'earn' the borrowing rate, and this is tax free. Positive balances in your current and savings accounts are set off against your most expensive borrowing first. You can link up to 80 different accounts.

SUPPORT: Local-rate helpline, 8am to 9pm, 7 days a week.

DOWNLOAD TO MONEY-MANAGEMENT SOFTWARE: Not at present.

CONTACT DETAILS: Under 'Help' you'll find a phone number and the address of the Halifax Registered Office. Dig deeper into 'Help – Privacy principles' and you'll even come across the address of the Intelligent Finance compliance officer.

PRIVACY: Details are given in question-and-answer format under 'Help'. If you want to keep a copy, you'll need separately to print off up to 30 Q&As. Usefully, you are given phone numbers for the Mailing, Phone, Fax and Email Preference Services so you can easily opt out of receiving junk mail and calls.

SECURITY AND LIABILITY: Easy to find under 'About us' and very comprehensive. When it comes to liability, the 'About us' page states Intelligent Finance guarantees that, if you are a victim of fraud, you will be reimbursed in full. This presumably overrides the out-of-date (2000) terms and conditions that we found on the site.

OTHER: Caters for special-needs users – for example if you are partially sighted, however not the most user-friendly site tested. Includes 'Quick quote' to work out how much you could save by using Intelligent Finance's combined account, but, despite the name, this facility is tediously slow to come up with a result. If you want to keep a record of the terms and conditions, be warned that the Adobe Acrobat file is slow to download and even slower to print – perhaps you should just wait for a copy in the Welcome pack. We also came across an error page in the Help section and annoyingly, instead of being able to click back to the previous page, had to close the window and relaunch 'Help'. Intelligent Finance also offers WAP phone banking.

## Lloyds-TSB
### www.lloydstsb.com

TYPE OF SERVICE: Option available with traditional bank accounts.

BASICS: As outlined on pages 62–9. You can view current and savings accounts.

SUPPORT: Local-rate helpline.

DOWNLOAD TO MONEY-MANAGEMENT SOFTWARE: Not at present.

CONTACT DETAILS: Phone numbers given, plus 'Branch locator' to help you find a bricks-and-mortar contact.

PRIVACY: You'll find this by following the 'Legal' link, which is in tiny print at the foot of the home page.

SECURITY AND LIABILITY: Clear link from the home page to a rather scant security policy, but useful tips. The conditions of use require you to follow the security rules set out in the User Guide, but as the User Guide does not appear to be on the web site, you'll have to sign up before you can find out whether or not the rules are reasonable. Provided you follow these unknown rules, you will not be liable for any loss due to fraudulent use of your account either before or after notifying the bank of a problem.

OTHER: Site includes large-type information for visually impaired people, but you'll need a magnifying glass to find the link to it (called 'Accessibility'), which sits in tiny print at the foot of the home page. Lloyds-TSB also offers interactive digital TV banking.

## Nationwide
### www.nationwide.co.uk

TYPE OF SERVICE: Option available with traditional bank accounts.

BASICS: As outlined on pages 62–9. Covers current and savings accounts. A special e-savings account offering a competitive savings rate is available only if you have an online current account. View the last 13 months' transactions.

SUPPORT: Local-rate helpline, 24 hours a day, 7 days a week.

DOWNLOAD TO MONEY-MANAGEMENT SOFTWARE: Microsoft Money.

CONTACT DETAILS: Address is given on the home page. Phone numbers readily found by following 'Contact us' and also under 'Help – features'. Branch locator also available.

PRIVACY: No privacy policy found.

SECURITY AND LIABILITY: Find a comprehensive security policy by following the 'Help – security' link from the Registration page. You are not liable for any loss due to unauthorised use of your account, provided you follow the security requirements set out in the terms and conditions. The requirements are reasonable.

OTHER: Site has a lot of extra features, including house price information, calculators and online shopping links. Nationwide also offers mobile banking using a pocket PC personal organiser (palm device).

---

## NatWest
## www.natwest.com

> ✕ – you are unacceptably exposed in the event of fraud.

TYPE OF SERVICE: Option available with traditional bank accounts.

BASICS: As outlined on pages 62–9. You can search for particular transactions.

SUPPORT: Local-rate helpline, 24 hours.

DOWNLOAD TO MONEY-MANAGEMENT SOFTWARE: Microsoft Money, Intuit Quicken, Sage and spreadsheets.

CONTACT DETAILS: Addresses given – right-click your mouse to print them off.

PRIVACY: No comprehensive privacy policy found. Some confidentiality information given under 'Important legal information' (right-click to print) and in the terms and conditions (which can be printed easily).

SECURITY AND LIABILITY: Security policy can be read from the Log-in screen (right-click your mouse to print). Worryingly it says: 'If a hacker gains access as a result of circumstances beyond NatWest's control ... NatWest is not liable.' This leaves you exposed, as quite likely the circumstances would also be beyond your control. The terms and conditions are just as frightening, stating: 'You will be liable for any unauthorised transactions which we carry out as a result of an instruction sent using your Security Codes.'

OTHER: NatWest is also an internet service provider (ISP) – the ISP service is free but you pay for calls. It also offers WAP phone banking.

---

## Norwich and Peterborough
## www.netmastergold.co.uk

TYPE OF SERVICE: Internet-only accounts from a traditional building society.

BASICS: As outlined on pages 62–9. Includes current and savings accounts, but you can also view certain other Norwich and Peterborough products (but not some passbook accounts and not your mortgage). Current account has a £500 free overdraft. You can view the last six months' transactions.

SUPPORT: Local-rate helpline, Monday to Friday 8am to 8pm, Saturday 9am to 5pm.

DOWNLOAD TO MONEY-MANAGEMENT SOFTWARE: Not at present.

CONTACT DETAILS: Admirably clear contact details giving the option to get in touch by phone or in writing, as well as by email.

PRIVACY: No privacy policy found.

SECURITY AND LIABILITY: Comprehensive security information given under 'Questions', with useful tips (right-click your mouse to print). You are liable for up to £50 of losses due to unauthorised use of your account, up to the time you notify the building society. Thereafter you are not liable provided you follow certain security conditions. These are fairly demanding and include: having up-to-date anti-virus software installed on your PC; not accessing the service from a PC you do not own (for example, a PC at work, in a cybercafé, at a library or a university); and not keeping any record of your password, even in disguised form.

OTHER: Site is well laid out with clear navigation and good download speeds. Useful account-switching service with preprinted letters if you want to transfer to Netmaster Gold.

---

## Royal Bank of Scotland
### www.rbos.co.uk

TYPE OF SERVICE: Option available with traditional bank accounts.

BASICS: As outlined on pages 62–9. Covers current and savings accounts, ISAs, tax-exempt special savings accounts (TESSAs), credit cards and mortgages. You can view up to 50 accounts, plus the last six months' transactions or search for specific transactions. There is a massive payee menu with more than 850 companies listed to help you set up bill-payment arrangements quickly. Payments can be arranged up to 120 days in advance. Direct Saver is a savings account offering competitive rates available only to online customers.

SUPPORT: Local-rate helpline, 8am to midnight, 7 days a week.

DOWNLOAD TO MONEY-MANAGEMENT SOFTWARE: Microsoft Money and Intuit Quicken, plus any packages that accept 'csv' format.

CONTACT DETAILS: 'Contact us' opens a new window with the addresses and phone numbers you need (right-click your mouse to print them off).

PRIVACY: You'll find a reasonably detailed privacy policy in the terms and conditions (again, you'll need to right-click your mouse to print these off).

SECURITY AND LIABILITY: A scant security policy is easily found from the home page, but for comprehensive detail go to the Questions section. Provided you have taken care to keep your security details secret, you are not liable for any loss due to unauthorised use of your account.

OTHER: Perhaps we just chose several bad days, but we were persistently dogged by windows that would not open and links that did not function or opened up the wrong material. The site speed was slow. Navigation was unhelpful with important information often buried several menus deep.

# Smile
## www.smile.co.uk

> ✓ – although it's a shame that consumer-friendly Smile could not run to a local-rate helpline

TYPE OF SERVICE: Co-operative Bank's dedicated Internet bank.

BASICS: As outlined on pages 62–9. Covers current and savings accounts, cash ISAs, credit cards and personal loans. The current account has a free £500 overdraft. Bill payments can be set up in advance.

SUPPORT: National-rate helpline, plus national-rate technical helpdesk, 8am to 10pm, 7 days a week.

DOWNLOAD TO MONEY-MANAGEMENT SOFTWARE: Not at present.

CONTACT DETAILS: Easily found with clear choice of writing or phoning, as well as email.

PRIVACY: Comprehensive privacy policy detailed in the terms and conditions.

SECURITY AND LIABILITY: There is some security information in the terms and conditions, details about the use of cookies is under 'Apply', but there is no clear statement in one place about the security measures the bank follows. However, at the time of writing, Smile was the only Internet bank to have been awarded a British kitemark for security. You are liable for a maximum of £50 of any loss due to unauthorised use of your account. The terms and conditions require that you do not write down your security codes.

OTHER: Very fast site, nicely laid out (especially if you like pink) and good, clear navigation. Site includes useful calculators, and there is a handy 'What you'll need' section that helps you gather together all the information required to fill in the application form. Preprinted letters help you transfer from another bank to Smile. As part of the Co-operative Bank, Smile follows an ethical policy that sets out which organisations the bank will and will not do business with.

## Virgin
## www.online.virgin-direct.co.uk

| ✕ – you are unacceptably exposed in the event of fraud. |
| --- |

TYPE OF SERVICE: Internet service is complementary to Virgin's direct phone services.

BASICS: As outlined on pages 62–9. Service covers all your Virgin products – current and savings account, credit cards, ISAs, unit trusts and so on. The only current account is part of Virgin One, which is a 'combined account' (see page 60). This means the interest rate you pay or receive is calculated on the combined balance of your current and savings accounts and borrowing via a mortgage, credit cards or personal loan. If you are a net borrower, your current and savings accounts effectively 'earn' the borrowing rate, and this is tax free. You can view the last 30 days' transactions or search for specific transactions. Details of the Virgin One account can be found at *www.virginone.co.uk*

SUPPORT: Local-rate helpline, 24 hours a day, 7 days a week.

DOWNLOAD TO MONEY-MANAGEMENT SOFTWARE: Not at present.

CONTACT DETAILS: 'Contact us' clearly sets out your options to phone or write, as well as email.

PRIVACY: No privacy policy found.

SECURITY AND LIABILITY: Easily found on the home page and can be readily printed off. The Conditions (on the Registration page) contain the following statement: 'You will be responsible for all instructions received by us ... Please note that this includes ... instructions sent by someone other than yourself ...'. This leaves you exposed to potentially large losses in the event of fraud.

OTHER: Download speeds good. Layout and navigation are clear, but the 'console'-type display is a matter of taste.

## Woolwich
## www.woolwich.co.uk

TYPE OF SERVICE: Option available with Open Plan account.

BASICS: As set out on pages 62–9. Open Plan is a combined account (see page 60). This means the interest rate you pay or receive is calculated on the combined balance of your current and savings accounts and any mortgage – you can also incorporate credit cards and personal loans. If you are a net borrower, your current and savings accounts effectively 'earn' the borrowing rate, and this is tax free. Open Plan can also be used as a 'sweeper account' (see page 60) – you set the maximum you want to hold in your current account, and any excess is automatically transferred to a special savings account. Any shortfall is made up by automatically transferring money back. You can view the last three years' transactions and arrange to pay bills up to 42 days in advance.

SUPPORT: Local-rate helpline.

DOWNLOAD TO MONEY-MANAGEMENT SOFTWARE: Microsoft Money.

CONTACT DETAILS: 'Contact us' gives you phone numbers and branches to visit. There is no centralised address to write to.

PRIVACY: The privacy policy is set out in the terms and conditions.

SECURITY AND LIABILITY: The security policy is detailed in the FAQ section. If your account is used without your consent, you are liable for a maximum loss of £50 before notifying the bank. After that, you are not liable provided you have complied with the security terms and conditions. These are generally reasonable but do require you not to keep a written record of your security details.

OTHER: Good, clear navigation. Transfer pack supplied to help you switch to Open Plan. The service is currently not available to Apple Mac users. Woolwich also offers WAP phone banking and interactive digital TV banking.

# Savings online

**6**

Savings accounts can meet a number of financial needs, for example:

- **an emergency fund** to draw on in a crisis, for example if you suddenly need to replace your car or make repairs to your home
- **short-term savings** to build up money over a short period (up to three years, say) to meet a particular expense, such as paying for a holiday or wedding, or saving up for a deposit on your own home
- **spreading your assets** – over the long term (five years or more), investments such as stocks and shares have tended to give a better return than savings accounts. But it is risky to put all your eggs in one basket, so having some of your money in savings accounts reduces your exposure if there is a dip in the stock market
- **a low-risk home for long-term savings** – if you are very uncomfortable with risk, you might decide to avoid the stock market altogether and rely completely on savings accounts. Although you'll usually get a lower return than from the stock market, you may save yourself sleepless nights
- **a temporary home for lump sums** – for example if you receive an inheritance or redundancy money and want to take a while deciding how best to use it.

## Choosing a savings account

The main factors to consider when choosing a savings account are how readily you can access your money and the return you'll get.

## Access

With some accounts you agree to leave your money invested for a set period or to give notice (for example, 30, 60 or 90 days) when you want to make a withdrawal. If the account offers a variable rate (ie, one that rises and falls with general interest rates), it is worth tying up your money in this way only if you are being offered a higher interest rate than that available on accounts that let you have your money back immediately without penalty (called 'instant access', 'easy access' or 'no-notice' accounts). If the account offers a fixed rate of interest, you might reckon it is worth tying up your money if you think general interest rates are likely to fall in future or you need the certainty of a fixed income.

## The return

Comparative tables, like the ones you'll find on many web sites, usually give the gross (before-tax) return. This may be the advertised rate or the 'annual equivalent rate' (AER). The AER takes into account how often interest is paid out or credited to your account. For example, suppose two accounts have an advertised rate of 5 per cent a year, but one credits the whole 5 per cent at the end of each year and the other credits you with 1.25 per cent every three months. The AER for the first account is simply 5 per cent. But the AER for the second account is 5.1 per cent because as soon as each three-monthly tranche of interest has been credited it too starts to earn interest, boosting your overall return. Using the AERs gives you a more accurate comparison.

When comparing accounts, it is important to look at the return you will get after the deduction of any tax. You will earn the gross rate of interest only if:

- **the product offers a tax-free return**, as is the case with cash individual savings accounts (ISAs), tax-exempt special savings accounts (TESSAs) and some National Savings products (National Savings Certificates, Children's Bonus Bonds and Premium Bonds), *or*
- **you are a non-taxpayer** – with many products, the interest is usually paid with 20 per cent tax already deducted.

You can arrange to receive the interest gross by completing form R85, available from banks, building societies and tax offices. You'll need to sign and post the form by mail.

If you are a starting-rate taxpayer, in 2001–2 you are liable for tax at only 10 per cent on any savings income that is not tax-free. If 20 per cent tax has already been deducted, you will need to reclaim part.

Non-taxpayers and starting-rate taxpayers who need to reclaim tax can do this either through their tax return, using a repayment claim form or form R40 from their tax office (you might be automatically sent a form each year).

If you are a basic-rate taxpayer, you are liable for 20 per cent tax on savings income. If this has already been deducted, you have no further tax to pay.

Higher-rate taxpayers pay tax at 40 per cent on savings income. If the interest is paid with 20 per cent tax already deducted, you have a further 20 per cent to pay, either through self-assessment or the Pay-As-You-Earn (PAYE) system.

## Using the Internet

There are two ways in which the Internet can help you choose the right savings accounts:

- some of the best returns are available with Internet-based accounts
- there are numerous web sites that sift through a huge selection of the accounts available and give you a shortlist of ones that may suit you. Because interest rates are constantly changing, it can be very hard to keep track of the market yourself, so these sites can be a handy, bang up-to-date alternative to checking the personal finance press and money magazines.

### Internet-only savings accounts

Internet-based accounts usually feature heavily in any list of best-buy savings accounts. However, many phone-based and postal accounts offer rates that are almost as good, and some of the front runners are available by a choice of routes, for example phone or Internet.

At the time of writing, all the Internet-only savings accounts were no-notice – in other words, you can make withdrawals whenever you want without giving any notice or losing any interest. The table overleaf compares the rates available in June 2001.

Many of the savings accounts listed in the table are available through the same web sites as the banking services described in Chapter 5, and so are covered by the same terms regarding security, privacy, contact details, and so on. Refer back to Chapter 5 to check out these features. See pages 97 to 101 of this chapter for details of web sites not included in Chapter 5.

## The Internet service

All online savings accounts work in broadly the same way as outlined below.

### Access

Usually you can view your accounts and transfer money to and from the account 24 hours a day, 7 days a week. However, instructions given outside normal banking hours are not usually carried out until the next working day.

### Paying money in and making withdrawals

Arrangements for paying money in do vary. Some accounts, such as First-e and Egg's standard account, accept cheques, but many do not. Where you are operating several accounts online from the same provider, you can usually make transfers yourself between the accounts, as described in Chapter 5. If you have a sweeper account (see page 60), surplus money in your current account can be automatically transferred to your savings account.

Another common arrangement is to make an initial payment into the savings account by cheque, but subsequent payments through the Banks Automated Clearing System (BACS). This is often achieved by designating one or more

## Returns on Internet-only savings accounts

| Bank or building society | See this page for details of the web site | Account | Before-tax % rate of interest paid on balance of: | | | |
| --- | --- | --- | --- | --- | --- | --- |
| | | | £1 | £1,000 | £10,000 | £100,000 |
| Abbey National | | | | | | |
| www.abbeynational.co.uk | p. 75 | eSaver | n/a | n/a | 5.9 | 5.9 |
| Bank of Scotland | | | | | | |
| www.bankofscotland.co.uk | p. 77 | i.save | 4.25 | 5.25 | 5.25 | 5.25 |
| Barclays Bank | | | | | | |
| www.barclays.co.uk | p. 77 | e-savings[1] | 1.55 | 1.55 | 4.50 | 5.00 |
| Bristol & West | | | | | | |
| www.bristol-west.co.uk | p. 98 | save.it | n/a | n/a | 4.75 | 4.75 |
| Egg | | | | | | |
| www.egg.com | p. 99 | Internet Savings | 5.25 | 5.25 | 5.25 | 5.25 |
| | | Investor[2] | 6.25 | 6.25 | 6.25 | 5.25 |
| First Direct | | | | | | |
| www.firstdirect.com | p. 80 | Savings | 2.18 | 2.91 | 4.65 | 5.03 |
| First-e | | | | | | |
| www.first-e.co.uk | p. 81 | Savings | 4.25 | 4.25 | 4.75 | 4.95 |
| Halifax | | | | | | |
| www.halifax-online.co.uk | p. 82 | Web Saver | 5.55 | 5.55 | 5.55 | 5.55 |
| Nationwide | | | | | | |
| www.nationwide.co.uk | p. 85 | e-Savings[1] | 5.55 | 5.55 | 5.55 | n/a |
| NatWest | | | | | | |
| www.natwest.com | p. 86 | e-Savings[1] | 4.2 | 4.2 | 4.75 | 5.1 |
| Newcastle | | | | | | |
| www.newcastlenet.co.uk | p. 100 | Net Savings | n/a | 5.3 | 5.8 | 5.8 |
| Norwich and Peterborough | | | | | | |
| www.netmastergold.co.uk | p. 87 | Netmaster Gold Saver[1] | 5.75 | 5.75 | 5.75 | n/a |
| Royal Bank of Scotland | | | | | | |
| www.rbos.co.uk | p. 88 | Direct Saver | 4.25 | 4.25 | 4.75 | 5.25 |
| Smile | | | | | | |
| www.smile.co.uk | p. 89 | Savings | 4.25 | 4.25 | 4.25 | 4.25 |

1. Available only if you have a current account with this bank/building society.
2. Available only if you have an Egg ISA.

*Source:* Moneyfacts, June 2001.

accounts – say your normal current account – and setting up a direct debit from that account. The direct debit is used as a channel to make BACS payments both into and out of the savings account. The designated accounts do not have to be online accounts; the only requirement is that they have a direct-debit facility. Usually the accounts must be in your own name – not in the name of your business or one that you hold as a trustee.

Depending on the savings account, other ways to pay in money might be by debit card or by one-off BACS transfers (without a direct-debit mandate).

Again, withdrawing money varies from one account to another. Some, such as Egg's Cashcard account, come with a card that you can use to make withdrawals at cash machines. Accounts operated by direct debit usually allow withdrawals only in the form of transfers to a designated account. Some accounts issue cheques sent to your home. With some providers cheques can be payable only to you; with others, they can be payable to a third party.

### Opening an account

Unless you already have an account with the bank or building society offering the savings account, you will normally have to post proof of your identity and address along with the completed application form (which you can print from the web site). If you already have an account, the proofs are not required and you may be able to open the account online.

### Logging in

From the log-in page, you usually need to type in an identification code and password in order to access your account. Each joint account holder has their own code and password.

### What you can do online

Typically, you can view your balance and most recent transactions. You may be able to call up a longer statement. You can transfer money into and out of your account either in one-off sums or as regular payments.

---

### Bristol & West
### www.bristol-west.co.uk

TYPE OF SERVICE: An online account, Save.it, from a largely bricks-and-mortar bank.

BASICS: Online savings account; minimum investment £10,000. Payments in and out are made by BACS from and to a designated account. If you hold the Save.it account jointly with someone else, you can each have a separate designated account. If you want to change the account you have designated, you need to do this in writing, not over the Internet. You can arrange for interest to be accumulated within the savings account or paid into your designated account on a monthly basis.

SUPPORT: Local-rate helpline, 8am to 10pm, 7 days a week. Bristol & West also has a 'direct service charter' under which it promises to respond to emails within 12 hours. If it fails to resolve your problem within 24 hours or makes a mistake, it will pay £10 into your account to compensate you for the inconvenience.

DOWNLOAD TO MONEY-MANAGEMENT SOFTWARE: Not at present.

CONTACT DETAILS: Link to a branch locator from the home page.

PRIVACY: No clear privacy statement. Some privacy details are covered in the 'Questions?' section.

SECURITY AND LIABILITY: Some security information is given in the terms and conditions, with further details in the 'Questions?' section. You are required not to write down your password (though, provided it is disguised, you can write down your personal security number). Although you appear to be liable in full for any losses that occur before you notify the bank that there is a problem, your exposure is in fact small. This is because withdrawals are made only to the designated account(s), and not to any third party.

OTHER: Also offers a range of other products that can be accessed online through its separate web site (*www.bristolandwestonline.co.uk*).

---

# Egg
## www.egg.com

TYPE OF SERVICE: Choice of Internet-only accounts and others that can be operated by Internet, phone and post.

BASICS: The Internet-only accounts offer the highest rates, but the top-paying Egg Savings (Investor) is open only to people who also have an Egg ISA. The Internet accounts let you pay in money by direct debit, BACS or debit card. Withdrawals are normally paid to a designated account. Other accounts have a wider choice of paying in and withdrawal options. With all accounts, you can view your balance and the last five transactions online, as well as giving transfer instructions.

SUPPORT: Local-rate helpline, 24 hours a day.

DOWNLOAD TO MONEY-MANAGEMENT SOFTWARE: Not at present.

CONTACT DETAILS: Easily found by following 'Contact us' from the home page.

PRIVACY: Once you locate the privacy policy (go to 'Savings' and then 'Legal information'), it is very clear and comprehensive.

SECURITY AND LIABILITY: Extremely clear and comprehensive information about the security arrangements Egg takes, together with useful tips on protecting yourself online. In general, you are liable without limit for any losses due to unauthorised use of your account during the period until you inform Egg that something is wrong. However, if the unauthorised use is due to computer fraud (rather than someone simply getting hold of your security details), Egg guarantees unconditionally to cover your losses.

OTHER: A clearly laid-out site with good navigation and a real attempt to give full information without any gobbledegook. You can also run Egg savings accounts by WAP phone and interactive digital TV.

---

## Newcastle

### www.newcastlenet.co.uk

TYPE OF SERVICE: Online account from a largely bricks-and-mortar building society.

BASICS: Payments in and out made via a direct-debit mandate with up to three designated accounts – initial investment by cheque. Changes to your nominated accounts must be made in writing rather than by Internet. Summary screen shows balances and mini-statements including the last five transactions, but you can opt to view earlier statements too.

SUPPORT: Standard phone number (area code 0191), Monday to Friday 8am to 8pm, Saturday 9am to 5pm, and Sunday 10am to 4pm.

DOWNLOAD TO MONEY-MANAGEMENT SOFTWARE: Microsoft Money and spreadsheets, such as Excel, that support 'csv' format.

CONTACT DETAILS: Follow 'Contact us' from the home page for addresses and phone numbers. Newcastle also operates a call-back service where, in response to your email, someone will call you by phone. You choose whether they call you straight away, in 15 minutes, or the same day at a time you specify.

PRIVACY: Only a statement in the terms and conditions of obligations under the Data Protection Act.

SECURITY AND LIABILITY: A brief security policy is outlined on the home page, with a bit more information in the FAQ section. You are liable without limit for losses due to unauthorised use of your account up to the time you tell Newcastle there is a problem. However, as withdrawals can be made only to your designated account(s) or by cheque to you at the address you registered with the service, the risk is probably fairly low.

OTHER: The service is not currently available to Apple Mac users. By opening an account you become a member of the building society. To deter 'carpetbaggers', you must agree that in the event of the building society being taken over or converting to a bank within five years of you opening an account, any windfall you would receive is given to charity.

## Other accounts available over the Net

As already noted in Chapter 5, many banks now give you the option of accessing bank services by a variety of means: at your branch, by phone and by Internet. This generally applies to savings accounts as well as a current account. To view and manage your savings accounts online, you need to sign up for the Internet service. You then choose whether or not to carry out a particular transaction online or via more traditional means. Banks offering the Internet as an option include:

- Alliance & Leicester, see page 76
- Bank of Scotland, see page 77
- Barclays, see page 77
- Citibank, see page 79
- Co-operative, see page 80
- Halifax, see page 82
- HSBC, see page 83

- Lloyds-TSB, see page 85
- Nationwide, see page 85
- NatWest, see page 86
- Royal Bank of Scotland, see page 88
- Virgin, see page 90
- Woolwich (Open Plan), see page 90.

## National Savings

You cannot operate National Savings investments online, but the National Savings web site (*www.nationalsavings.co.uk*) is the definitive source of information about these. There you'll find comprehensive information, tools to help you choose between the products, and prospectuses that you can print off.

## The Internet as a tool to help you choose a savings account

For raw data, one of the best sites is *www.moneyfacts.co.uk* Moneyfacts is a specialist independent company that collects and publishes comparative information on a wide range of financial products. When it comes to savings, Moneyfacts offers two useful options:

- **selections** For each type of account (for example no-notice, Internet-only, mini-cash ISA), the top six accounts are summarised
- **search** You specify the type of account you want and the average balance you expect to keep in the account. Moneyfacts then comes back with a comprehensive list of available accounts ranked by interest rate.

For each account you are interested in, you can click on 'Contact' and send your details to the provider with instructions to contact you.

You can also find searchable databases of savings accounts on various personal finance sites (the list overleaf provides a few suggestions). These usually have much the same format as the Moneyfacts search tool – you specify the type of account and amount you want to save.

- *uk.finance.yahoo.com*
- *www.ftyourmoney.com*
- *www.moneyextra.com*
- *www.lineone.net*
- *www.msn.co.uk*

Some personal finance web sites – for example *www.thisis-money.com*, *www.iii.co.uk* and *www.uk-invest.com* – do not have a search facility but list best-buy accounts, often showing the return you would get after tax.

## Background information

For an introduction to how savings accounts fit into your wider financial planning, try the Financial Services Authority (FSA)* consumer web site: *www.fsa.gov.uk/consumer*. For useful background articles on savings, try *www.which.net* and *www.iii.co.uk*.

# Investment funds and pensions online

**7**

If you have money to invest for the medium to long term (say, five years or more), it usually makes sense to put at least part of it into investments where the return is linked to shares. Over the medium to long term, shares have tended to outperform deposits (such as bank and building society accounts) by a handsome margin – see the chart overleaf. And, if you are saving for a very long-term goal – such as providing an income when you retire – you would have to set aside a dauntingly large sum if you relied only on deposits for growth.

However, the higher expected return on shares comes hand-in-hand with extra risk. The value of shares can fall as well as rise. By investing for the medium to long term, you should be able to ride out any dips in the market. But, if you can invest only for a few years, or may need your money back at short notice, shares are not a suitable option for you, as the market could be in the doldrums when you need to withdraw your funds.

Situations in which share-based investments are often a suitable choice include:

- saving for retirement
- saving for school fees or the cost of going to university, assuming there is at least five years until your children start this stage of their education
- building a nest-egg over a longish period of time
- investing a lump sum – for example an inheritance – that you will not need to use for at least five years.

## Value of a £1,000 investment after five years and ten years (income reinvested)

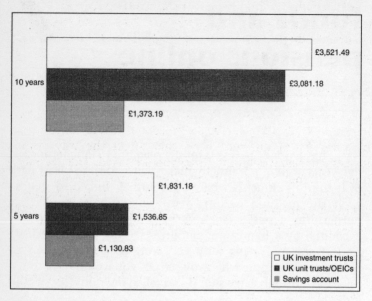

10 years

£3,521.49

£3,081.18

£1,373.19

5 years

£1,831.18

£1,536.85

£1,130.83

☐ UK investment trusts
■ UK unit trusts/OEICs
▨ Savings account

*Source*: *Money Management*, July 2001.

## Why choose an investment fund?

Investing in the shares of just one or two companies is risky. If one company suffered a bad patch, a fall in its share price could have a big impact on your wealth. To guard against this, you should spread your money across a portfolio of many different shares – a fall in the price of one would then have only a small impact on your total investment.

When you buy and sell shares, you must generally pay commission and, in the case of buying, stamp duty. These costs make small holdings of shares uneconomic. You should normally plan to invest at least £1,000 to £1,500 in each company whose shares you hold. All told, if you invest direct in shares, to have anything approaching a reasonably balanced portfolio, you'll need a stake of at least £10,000 to £15,000.

Holding shares direct can also be onerous because you need to deal with the administration of shareholder voting, possible rights issues, takeovers, and so on, as well as the work involved in making your purchases and sales.

All in all, buying into a readymade portfolio – an investment fund – is a simpler way to hold a broad spread of shares (or other investments), especially if you have relatively small sums to invest.

## Types of investment fund

All investment funds are portfolios of shares and/or other investments. But they can be packaged and sold to consumers in a variety of different ways that affect the way your investment behaves and the way you are taxed. This section briefly outlines how each type of fund works, and the main features are summarised in table on page 112. For more detailed information, follow the leads suggested in 'Background information and choosing a fund' on page 113.

### *Unit trusts*

With unit trusts, the investment fund is divided into equal segments called units.

You invest by buying the units. If there are more investors wanting to buy than sell, the investment fund grows, and more units are created. If more investors want to sell than buy, the fund shrinks, and units are cancelled. A fund that behaves like this is called 'open-ended'. The value of the units directly reflects the value of the underlying fund.

Usually, the price at which you buy units (the 'offer price') is higher than the price at which you sell (the 'bid price'). The difference between the two prices is a cost to you called the 'initial charge' or 'front-end load'. The initial charge is typically around 5 per cent, and a large part of it is used to pay commission to advisers and brokers. You also pay an annual management charge, which is a percentage of the value of your investments (often 1 to 1.5 per cent a year) and deducted from the fund. Some unit trusts charge an 'exit fee' if you cash in your investment within the first few years.

Other costs, such as commission for buying and selling the investments in the fund and paying a custodian to hold the assets safely, are deducted from the investment fund.

Your return from a unit trust can be made up of regular payments of income, called 'distributions', and a capital gain if you sell at a profit. Distributions are paid with 10 per cent tax already deducted, and non-taxpayers cannot reclaim this. Starting-rate and basic-rate taxpayers have no further tax to pay. Higher-rate taxpayers are taxed at a rate of 32.5 per cent but can set a 10 per cent tax credit against this.

## Open-ended investment companies (OEICs)

From the investor's point of view, OEICs are very similar to unit trusts. Technically they are different because they are companies rather than trusts. European investors are more comfortable with the company structure, so providers who want to attract an international clientele are tending to offer OEICs instead of unit trusts.

You invest by buying shares in the company. If there are more buyers than sellers, extra shares are created. If there are more sellers than buyers, shares are cancelled. In this way, the fund is 'open-ended' and the value of the shares directly reflects the value of the investments in the fund.

There is a single price at which you buy and sell the shares. Any initial charge (typically around 5 per cent) is shown separately. There is also an annual management charge (typically 1 to 1.5 per cent a year), which is deducted from the fund. Some OEICs charge an 'exit fee' if you cash in your investment within the first few years.

Other costs, such as commission for buying and selling the investments in the fund and paying a custodian to hold the assets safely, are deducted from the investment fund.

Returns from OEICs are treated in the same way as unit trusts (see above).

## Investment trusts

Investment trusts are also companies that run an investment fund, and you invest by buying shares in the company.

Unlike OEICs, investment trusts are 'closed-ended funds'. This means that regardless of the number of buyers and sellers, the number of shares issued stays exactly the same. Instead, the relative balance of buyers and sellers affects the price of the shares. If there are more buyers than sellers, the share price tends to rise. If there are more sellers than buyers, the share price tends to fall. As a result, the price of the shares is not directly linked to the value of assets in the investment fund, but also reflects demand for the shares.

Investment trusts are quoted on the stock exchange. You buy the shares either through a stockbroker or direct from the provider. Except where the shares are being newly issued, you pay commission to the stockbroker you use. If you have gone direct to the provider, your order will still go through a stock-broker, but the commission might be a bit lower because the provider can pool your order with those of other investors and perhaps get a discount for buying in bulk. Stockbrokers' commission must also be paid when you sell. Stamp duty (at ½ per cent) is charged on purchases but not sales.

As with most shares, there is a difference (called the 'spread') between the price you buy at and the price you can sell at – this is in effect another charge for you to pay. The spread is usually fairly small.

In addition, the company charges an annual fee for managing the investment fund. This is typically around 0.5 to 1 per cent a year of the value of the fund, and is deducted from it.

Other costs, such as commission for buying and selling the investments in the fund and paying a custodian to hold the assets safely, are deducted from the investment fund.

Your return from an investment trust can be made up of dividends and a capital gain if you sell at a profit. Dividends are paid with 10 per cent tax already deducted, and non-taxpayers cannot reclaim this. Starting-rate and basic-rate taxpayers have no further tax to pay. Higher-rate taxpayers are taxed at a rate of 32.5 per cent but can set a 10 per cent tax credit against this.

Other differences between investment trusts and OEICs or unit trusts include:

- **gearing** – investment trusts can borrow money to buy assets that make up the investment fund. If the assets perform well, this practice magnifies the return to investors. If the assets do badly, it magnifies the losses. So gearing increases the potential return but also the risk

- **different types of shares** – investment trusts often have more than one class of share. Split-capital trusts have a set lifetime, after which the trust is wound up, and offer capital shares that receive the value of the assets at wind up (but no dividends in the meantime) and income shares that receive dividends during the life of the trust (but little or no capital on wind up). Zero-dividend preference shares ('zeros') receive no income but a set amount of capital on wind up (assuming the assets are sufficient) and are paid before any other class of shareholder, making them less risky than other types of investment trust share.

## Exchange traded funds (ETFs)

ETFs have been established in the US for several years, but are relatively new to the UK. Basically they are a cross between unit trusts and investment trusts.

An ETF is a company that usually invests in a fund designed to track a stock market index – for example the FTSE 100. You invest by buying the shares of the company, and these are quoted on a stock exchange. But, unlike investment trusts, the number of shares is not fixed. If sellers exceed buyers, shares can be redeemed by the company. If buyers exceed sellers, new shares can be issued. In other words, an ETF is an 'open-ended fund' and the price of the shares should closely reflect the value of the underlying investments in the fund.

You buy and sell ETF shares through a stockbroker to whom you pay commission. There is usually no stamp duty when you buy the ETF shares currently available in the UK. The spread between the price at which you buy and sell is usually very small. The company charges an annual fee for managing the investment fund, and this is deducted from income before it is paid out to investors. The fee is typically low because the fund is a tracker fund rather than an actively managed one (see Glossary).

Other costs, such as commission for buying and selling the investments in the fund and paying a custodian to hold the assets safely, are deducted from the investment fund.

ETFs do not usually borrow to buy assets, so there is no

gearing effect (unlike investment trusts).

Your return from an ETF can be made up of dividends and a capital gain if you sell at a profit. Tax is treated as per investment trusts (see above).

## Individual savings accounts (ISAs)

ISAs are not an investment as such, but a wrapper that you can put around a variety of savings and investments. The return from the investments in an ISA are free of income tax and capital gains tax.

There are three types of ISA:

- **cash ISA** for deposits such as bank and building society accounts
- **insurance ISA** for investment-type insurance policies
- **stocks-and-shares ISA** for shares, corporate bonds, gilts and many types of investment fund. Unit trusts, OEICs, investment trusts and ETFs can all be held within a stocks-and-shares ISA.

Each tax year, you can either have one of each type of ISA – called 'mini-ISAs' – or a single maxi-ISA that must have a stocks-and-shares component and can also include cash and insurance components. The maximum you can invest each year is shown in the table overleaf. You cannot take out both a maxi-ISA and mini-ISAs in the same tax year. If you want to invest more than £3,000 in stocks and shares (including investment funds), you must choose a maxi-ISA.

Many investment funds are marketed as ISAs – in other words, with the ISA wrapper automatically included. But you can also opt to invest in the fund without the ISA wrapper.

**Maximum you can invest in ISAs each tax year[1]**

| Type of ISA | Maximum you can invest |
| --- | --- |
| *You can choose up to three mini-ISAs, one each of:* | |
| Cash mini-ISA | £3,000 |
| Insurance mini-ISA | £1,000 |
| Stocks-and-shares mini-ISA | £3,000 |
| *Or you can have one maxi-ISA investing in the following components:* | |
| Cash component | £3,000 |
| Insurance component | £1,000 |
| Stocks-and-shares component | £7,000 less the amount, if any, you invest in any cash component and/or |
| insurance | component |

1. These limits apply until 5 April 2005, but may be changed thereafter.

## Personal equity plans (PEPs)

The forerunner of the stocks-and-shares ISA was the PEP. PEPs are a wrapper around shares, corporate bonds, investment funds, and so on. The return from investments within the PEP wrapper are free of income tax and capital gains tax.

You can no longer start a new PEP, but you can continue any PEPs you had already started before 6 April 1999, and you can transfer a PEP from one fund manager to another.

## Pension plans and schemes

The government encourages you to save for your retirement by giving various tax breaks when you save or invest through an approved pension plan or scheme.

- you get tax relief on what you pay in
- a large part of the return from investing your money is tax free
- you can take part of the proceeds as a tax-free lump sum.

The money you pay in is usually put into an investment fund (though can be invested direct in shares – see page 136). As with ISAs and PEPs, you can view the pension scheme or plan as a tax-free wrapper around your investment fund.

## The Enterprise Investment Scheme (EIS)

You are eligible for tax breaks when you invest in the new shares of small and growing unlisted trading companies that qualify for the EIS.

- there is 20 per cent income tax relief on investments up to £150,000 a year, provided you invest for at least three years
- any gain when you sell the shares is tax free, provided you invest for at least three years
- any loss when you sell the shares can be set against other gains or income
- tax on gains made on other assets can be deferred if you invest the gain in EIS shares.

Investors commonly buy the shares of a single EIS company, but you can also invest through a fund where your money is pooled with that of other investors and used to invest in several companies. EIS funds usually have an initial charge – say 7 per cent of your investment.

## Venture capital trusts (VCTs)

VCTs are basically a type of investment trust – a company quoted on the stock exchange that runs an investment fund – but they invest only in the shares of unlisted trading companies (the same sort of companies that can qualify for the EIS). If you invest in the newly issued shares of a VCT, you are eligible for various tax advantages.

- there is 20 per cent income tax relief on an investment up to £100,000 a year
- there is tax relief on dividends paid out by the VCT by deducting the tax credit accompanying the dividend from your tax bill for the year
- any gain when you sell the shares is tax free
- tax on gains made on other assets can be deferred if you invest the gain in VCT shares.

## Investment funds compared

| | Unit trusts | OEICs | Investment trusts | Exchange traded funds | ISAs | PEPs | Pension schemes and plans | EIS fund | VCTs |
|---|---|---|---|---|---|---|---|---|---|
| Price you pay is directly related to value of fund (ie open-ended fund) | Yes | Yes | No | Yes | 1 | 1 | 1 | Yes | No |
| Usually an initial charge (front-end load) | Yes | Yes | No | No | 1 | 1 | 1 | Yes | No |
| Spread between prices at which you buy and sell | Yes (includes initial charge) | No | Yes | Yes, but small | 1 | 1 | 1 | No | Yes |
| Annual management charge | Yes | Yes | Yes | Yes | Yes | Yes | Yes | Yes | Yes |
| Sometimes an exit charge | Yes | Yes | No | No | 1 | 1 | Yes | No | No |
| Dividends or distribution are taxable | Yes | Yes | Yes | Yes | No | No | Yes | Yes | No[2] |
| Capital gain is taxable | Yes | Yes | Yes | Yes | No | No | No | No | No |
| Tax relief on amount you invest | No | No | No | No | No | No | Yes | Yes | Yes |

1. Depends on type of fund inside the wrapper.
2. Unless you are a non-taxpayer, in which case you have no tax bill to set the tax credit against.

## Background information and choosing a fund

Below are signposted some of the most useful web sites if you are looking for background information or guidance choosing between different providers' funds. You may also find some other Which? Books* helpful, in particular *Which? Way to Save and Invest* for information about different types of investment, and *Be Your Own Financial Adviser* for guidance on how various investments can help you reach your financial goals.

Another useful background source is the FSA's* consumer web site (*www.fsa.gov.uk/consumer*), which includes FAQs on most types of investment and a guide to shopping around. From the second half of 2001, the FSA is also due to launch comparative information tables that, for some investment funds, will list the main features of each provider's product and allow you to produce shortlists according to the features you are interested in. The FSA's tables will not include performance data.

### Unit trusts and OEICs

The Association of Unit Trusts and Investment Funds (AUTIF)* is the trade body for these types of fund. Its web site (*www.investmentfunds.org.uk*) includes useful factsheets detailing how unit trusts and OEICs work, and how you can use them in your financial planning (go to the 'About funds' section). This section also includes a search engine to direct you towards suitable funds, given your answers to the following:

- the amount you have to invest
- whether you want an ISA, PEP, and so on
- whether you are seeking growth, income, or both
- whether you are interested in a particular sector (for example the UK, Japan, smaller companies)
- whether you have a particular provider in mind.

You can use the outcome of the search to check basic details about the particular funds, including contact information. The site also includes an A–Z listing of all the providers, providing another route for checking these details. With the majority of providers you can follow a link direct to their web site.

Several personal finance sites have good background information and similar search tools to help you choose a fund. They include Interactive Investor (*www.iii.co.uk*), MoneyeXtra (*www.moneyextra.com*) and Motley Fool (*www.fool.co.uk*).

## Investment trusts

The Association of Investment Trust Companies (AITC) is the trade body for investment trusts. Its site (*www.aitc.co.uk*) is divided into two sections. 'About ITS' contains clear and useful guides on how investment trusts work. 'Buying ITS' includes information on how to buy and links to stockbrokers (for more about stockbrokers, see Chapter 8).

The 'Buying ITS' section also includes a 'Trustfinder' that shortlists suitable investment trusts, given information you provide on the following:

- whether you're saving for growth, income, or both
- your attitude towards risk
- the type of trust you're interested in – for example global, smaller companies, UK high income
- whether you're looking for an ISA, savings scheme, pension, and so on
- how much you can invest.

There is also a list of investment trusts with details and links to their web sites.

Other sources of background information include Interactive Investor (*www.iii.co.uk*), Motley Fool (*www.fool.co.uk*) and, if you are interested in split-capital trusts, *www.splitsonline.co.uk*

## ETFs

At present there are relatively few ETFs available in the UK, and not many sites include information about them. The best source is *www.ishares.net*, run by the provider behind the majority of ETFs currently quoted on the London Stock Exchange.

## ISAs and PEPs

Where you find information about unit trusts, OEICs and investment trusts, you'll invariably also find information on ISAs and PEPs, so try *www.investmentfunds.co.uk* and *www.aitc.co.uk* to start with. Also visit general personal finance web sites, such as *www.iii.co.uk*, *www.ftyourmoney.co.uk* and *www.fool.co.uk*

For the last word on tax treatment, go to the Inland Revenue\* web site (*www.inlandrevenue.gov.uk*). ISAs are featured in the 'Individuals' section.

## Pension schemes and plans

There is a lot of general information on the Web about pension planning and the broad types of schemes and plans available – see, for example, the government site at *www.pensionguide.gov.uk*, the FSA at *www.fsa.gov.uk/consumer*, and general personal finance web sites such as *www.iii.co.uk*, *www.ftyourmoney.co.uk* and *www.thisismoney.com*

For the tax treatment of pensions, go to the Inland Revenue web site (*www.inlandrevenue.gov.uk*).

## The EIS

For a brief introduction, try the web site of the Enterprise Investment Scheme Agency (EISA) (*www.eisa.org.uk*). You can follow a link from there to the Inland Revenue site, or go to the Revenue's site (*www.inlandrevenue.gov.uk*) under your own steam, where in the 'Leaflets and booklets' section ('Business – General') you'll find booklet IR137 about the EIS.

However, information on the Internet is scant, and EIS investments are high-risk, so you would be well advised to get face-to-face advice from an independent financial adviser (IFA). To find an IFA, see Chapter 13.

## VCTs

Brief information is available on the web site of the British Venture Capital Association (BVCA) (*www.bvca.co.uk*). For tax information, go to the Inland Revenue web site (*www.inlandrevenue.gov.uk*). You'll find leaflet IR169 about

VCTs by following this route: 'Leaflets and booklets'/'Business' – 'General'. Once again, you are looking at a high-risk investment, and it would be sensible to get personal advice from an IFA.

## Performance data and other fund details

A great deal of research has been done by both academics and specialist investment firms to test whether the past performance of a fund is a useful factor in helping you to choose a fund which will do well in future. Since investment performance will undoubtedly turn out to be the most important determinant of the return you get from your investment, it would be very handy if there was some way of predicting which funds are likely to do well. Unfortunately, all the different research studies tend to come to the same conclusions:

- over the medium to long term, there is no correlation between funds that have done well in the past and funds that do well in the future
- there may be a very weak link between firms that have done badly in the past and those that do badly or close down in the future.

Therefore, it may be sensible to avoid the very worst performing funds, but otherwise past performance data unfortunately appears to be no use at all in helping you choose where to put your money. Despite this and the warning in all ads that 'the past is no guide to the future', investors are often still keen to check out past performance, so we have included here some sites that provide this information.

### Unit trusts, OEICs and investment trusts

One of the most comprehensive sites is *www.trustnet.co.uk* As well as price and performance data for unit trusts and OEICs, the site includes similar data for conventional and split-capital investment trusts, as well as investment trust warrants. It also has a portfolio tracker tool that you can use to keep tabs on whatever funds, indices and shares you choose to key in.

If you are investing in split-capital investment trusts, *www.splitsonline.co.uk* is the definitive site and includes details of current share price, redemption price and yield, cover and hurdle rates.

See also *www.funds-sp.com*, the fund data site run by Standard & Poors.

## ISAs and PEPs

Some sites focus on unit trusts and OEICs ready packaged in the ISA wrapper, for example MoneyeXtra (*www.moneyextra.com*), and this is often coupled with a buying online service (see below).

## Pensions

The *www.funds-sp.com* site includes performance data for UK pension funds.

### The EIS

To qualify for the EIS tax benefits, you must invest in newly issued shares, so it is in the nature of the investment that offers are on the table for a relatively short period of time. For a list of EIS opportunities currently available, visit the independent financial adviser Best Invest (*www.bestinvest.co.uk*).

### VCTs

Best Invest (*www.bestinvest.co.uk*) also lists VCT opportunities currently on offer. These are also available from the BVCA site (*www.bvca.co.uk*).

## Buying investment funds online

The UK has a long way to go before you will be able to buy and sell all your investments online. In practice, many web sites give information only, and require you to phone if you are ready to buy. Others provide a halfway house that lets you complete an application form online, which must then be printed and posted. Relatively few sites allow you to complete the whole buying process online. Those that do are, in the main, selling unit trusts and OEICs with or without the ISA wrapper. A few investment trusts can be bought from the provider online, but, like any other shares, all investment trusts can be bought through stockbrokers – see Chapter 8 for details of online broking services.

## Buying direct

The table below lists providers offering an online service.

Before buying direct from the provider, check whether you can get a cheaper deal from a 'fund supermarket' – see opposite.

## Fund supermarkets

A fund supermarket is a single web site where you can browse through and buy investment funds offered by a range of different providers. Broadly they work in either of two ways:

- **true supermarkets** – the web site provider offers the whole package, arranging your investments and, if you

### Unit trust providers offering an online dealing service

**Web site**

| | |
|---|---|
| www.abbeynational.co.uk | www.martincurrie.com |
| www.aberdeen-asset.com | www.mlim.co.uk |
| www.abetterway.co.uk | www.norwich-union.co.uk |
| www.ArtemisOnline.co.uk | www.perpetual.co.uk |
| www.barclaysfunds.co.uk | www.rsainvestments.com |
| www.britannicasset.com | www.sarasin.co.uk |
| www.chaseflemingam.co.uk | www.schroders.co.uk |
| www.csamfunds.co.uk | www.scottishamicable.co.uk |
| www.edfd.com | www.scottishfriendly.co.uk |
| www.equitable.co.uk | www.scottishmutual.co.uk |
| www.fidelity.co.uk | www.scottishwidows.co.uk |
| www.gartmore.com | www.singer.co.uk |
| www.govett.co.uk | www.teachers-group.co.uk |
| www.investecfunds.co.uk | www.standardlifeinvestments.co.uk |
| www.jupiteronline.co.uk | www.stewartivory.co.uk |
| www.landg.com | www.threadneedle.co.uk |
| www.leggmasoninvestors.com | www.virgin-direct.co.uk |
| www.mandg.co.uk | www.wesleyan.co.uk |
| www.marksandspencer.com/ financialservices | www.woolwich.co.uk |

are using the ISA wrapper, allowing you to put funds from several providers within the same ISA. An advantage is that you need just one set of security details to access all the investments made through the supermarket. The largest true supermarket is FundsNetwork run by Fidelity

- **quasi-supermarkets** – the web site brings together information about different providers' products and may make special offers, but for purchase you transfer to individual providers' web sites. This means you have different security arrangements with each provider. Usually any ISA is operated by the individual fund provider and so contains only that provider's funds.

Some fund supermarkets are operated by a fund provider that also offers the products of its rivals. So far these supermarkets operate on a no-advice basis only. There may be a questionnaire to establish broadly what type of fund you are looking for and generate a shortlist of potentially suitable funds, but this falls short of advice (which would need to take into account your own particular personal and financial circumstances). The ultimate choice is yours alone, and you should buy this way only if you feel confident about your decision.

Other fund supermarkets are run by independent financial advisers or stockbrokers. In this case, you are often offered the choice of seeking advice or buying direct without advice. CharcolOnline and Wise up offer automated advice services that generate specific recommendations about the fund(s) you should buy.

What all fund supermarkets have in common is that they act like discount brokers. Instead of taking the full commission offered by a fund provider, they forgo a large part of it, which typically reduces the initial charge you pay. Some give up all the initial commission, which reduces the initial charge typically to around 0.25 per cent, or even nothing at all. (An investment fund with no initial charge is often referred to as a 'no-load fund'.) For this reason you will usually pay less by going to a fund supermarket than you will buying direct from the provider. However, you may still pay more using a fund supermarket than you would going to a discount broker.

Offline, discount brokers frequently offer funds with no initial charge *and* a reduction in the annual management fee.

You should be aware that when you use a fund supermarket you are liable for any unauthorised access to your investment prior to telling the provider that there is a problem. None of the supermarkets we looked at limited your liability to a set amount, and some are quite clear that the liability is yours even if you can prove that you were not to blame.

Details of the main fund supermarkets available to UK investors are given below. In the US, fund supermarkets have been around for some time, and just two supermarkets account for around 90 per cent of all the business. If the UK follows the same pattern, only one or two fund supermarkets are eventually likely to dominate.

---

## AMP
## www.ample.co.uk

Type of service: True supermarket offering over 400 funds from 22 providers. Funds can be held in Ample ISAs or PEPs. The site includes extensive support material, including news, fund statistics, prices, fund factsheets and portfolio tracker.
Charges: Majority have 1 per cent initial charge, some up to 1.5 per cent.
Advice: Fund selector to help you to choose suitable funds, though this falls short of advice. You can opt to delegate your fund management to Henderson, an AMP subsidiary.

---

## BestInvest
## www.bestinvest.co.uk

Type of service: A quasi-supermarket from independent financial adviser BestInvest. You can buy online either by following a link to FundsNetwork (see page 122) or through links to ISA providers that offer online dealing.
Charges: No initial commission.
Advice: You can use the tools to help you buy online without advice. Alternatively, you can choose to receive advice from BestInvest.

## CharcolOnline
**www.charcolonline.co.uk**

TYPE OF SERVICE: True fund supermarket offering choice of 250 funds from 18 providers within an ISA wrapper. You must first open a savings account with CharcolOnline, which provides the money for your fund purchases.
CHARGES: Nil to 1.5 per cent initial charge.
ADVICE: Automated online advice provided through the 'Fund adviser' service, which is free (though you must register). The site also includes a 'Financial health check' to sort out your overall financial planning.

## Chase de Vere
**www.chasedevere.co.uk**

TYPE OF SERVICE: Web site of one of the leading discount brokers. It provides a link to FundsNetwork (see page 000) for online dealing and offers discounts on some of the 180 funds from 27 unit trust and OEIC managers on offer through the site.
CHARGES: Reduced initial charge on some funds.
ADVICE: You can buy online without advice, or contact Chase de Vere by phone if you would prefer advice.

## Cheap Funds
**www.cheapfunds.co.uk**

TYPE OF SERVICE: The web site of stockbrokers Hichens, Harrison & Co plc. This is a quasi-supermarket offering discounts on around 1,800 unit trusts and OEICs. You can pay online for some of these using your debit card. A sister site, *www. agencyisa.co.uk*, focuses on unit trust and OEIC ISAs, with no initial charge.
CHARGES: No initial charge.
ADVICE: Tools to help you make your choice, but no advice.

## Egg
**www.egg.com**

TYPE OF SERVICE: Egg was the first fund supermarket to open in the UK. At the time of writing you can choose among 250 funds offered by 24 different unit trust managers. You can hold the funds of more than one manager in an Egg ISA. All instructions about buying and selling your units must be given by Internet. To use its fund supermarket, you have first to open an Egg savings account, which is used to finance your fund purchases. So far, Egg savings accounts have offered some of the highest interest rates available.

CHARGES: With most funds, the initial charge is no more than 1.5 per cent.

ADVICE: The site includes a variety of tools to help you choose your funds and manage your investments, but these do not constitute advice. You buy on a no-advice basis.

## Funds Direct
## www.fundsdirect.co.uk

TYPE OF SERVICE: Comprehensive true supermarket covering over 1,500 funds from more than 90 providers. You can hold funds direct or through a Funds Direct ISA. Site also includes news, fund statistics, fund factsheets and portfolio tracker.

CHARGES: Vary from nil to around 2.75 per cent.

ADVICE: Fund search facility but no advice.

## FundsNetwork
## www.fidelity.co.uk

TYPE OF SERVICE: FundsNetwork is run by Fidelity, itself an investment fund provider and the largest operator in the world of fund supermarkets. At the time of writing, FundsNetwork offers a choice of 500 funds from 34 unit trust managers. You can buy online, paying with a debit card. Funds from more than one provider can be put in a single Fidelity ISA wrapper. FundsNetwork also accepts PEP transfers.

CHARGES: All funds are offered at a discount. Some have no initial charge, many 1.25 per cent and a few up to 2.5 per cent.

ADVICE: A range of tools help you choose your funds and manage them, but there is no advice.

## Hargreaves Lansdown
### www.hargreaveslansdown.co.uk

TYPE OF SERVICE: Web site of one of the leading discount brokers. It offers an online ISA supermarket through a link to FundsNetwork (see opposite). Hargreaves Lansdown has negotiated reduced initial charges with the participating providers.

CHARGES: Some funds with no initial charge. The rest range from 0.25 to 1.25 per cent, with a few at 2 or 2.5 per cent.

ADVICE: Research material onsite, plus Hargreaves Lansdown's shortlist of favourite funds, but no advice.

## Interactive Investor
### www.iii.co.uk

TYPE OF SERVICE: This is a quasi-supermarket. Tools let you search the whole market for suitable funds. Interactive Investor has agreed discounts on around 400 funds from over 30 unit trust managers. To buy, you link to the individual providers, some of whom offer online dealing.

CHARGES: Discounts available on many funds.

ADVICE: Site contains a premium-rate helpline if you need financial advice. This puts you through to an IFA with whom Interactive Investor has a partnership.

## Inter-alliance
### www.inter-alliance.co.uk

TYPE OF SERVICE: A quasi-supermarket offering unit trusts, OEICs and investment trusts with or without the ISA wrapper. To buy, you link to the individual fund providers' sites. However, Inter-Alliance does offer its own ISA, into which you can put funds from more than one provider.

CHARGES: Initial charges reduced by up to 5 per cent.

ADVICE: Tools to help you choose, but no advice.

## TQ Direct Choice
### www.tqonline.co.uk

TYPE OF SERVICE: Web site of independent financial adviser Torquil Clark. Through a link to FundsNetwork (see page 122), it currently offers only online ISAs, but is planning to add other products. The supermarket also accepts PEP transfers.

CHARGES: In many cases the initial charge is reduced to 0.25 per cent.

ADVICE: No advice.

## Virginmoney
### www.virginmoney.com

TYPE OF SERVICE: This is a quasi-supermarket, with the Virginmoney site helping you choose an ISA but passing you on to the individual provider to complete the deal. If you choose a provider that is one of Virginmoney's 'e-associates' you get a special deal on charges. Some of the e-associates let you buy online; with others you simply register and receive an application pack by post.

CHARGES: No initial charge with any of the funds offered by the e-associates.

ADVICE: Tools help you select your ISA, but no advice is given.

## Wise up
### www.wiseup.co.uk

TYPE OF SERVICE: This site is run by independent financial adviser Bates Investment Services. It offers online purchase of ISAs through a link to FundsNetwork (see page 122).

CHARGES: Many initial charges reduced to 0.25 per cent; some have a higher charge and some no initial charge at all.

ADVICE: Includes an 'Auto advice' service. You answer a series of questions, for example about your tax status, whether you have an emergency fund, how long you can invest, your attitude towards risk, and how much you can invest. This is a bit more detailed than the fund-finder sections on most other web sites. The Wise up service recommends specific ISAs based on the answers you give. The recommended funds are contained in a 'reason why' letter that you can print off.

# Buying pensions online

## Buying direct

Pensions are relatively complicated products which have traditionally been sold with advice. This is changing with the introduction of stakeholder pensions from April 2001 onwards. Stakeholder pensions are straightforward, low-charging products that are intended to be accessible without advice. Instead, the pre-sale information includes 'decision trees' to provide you with guidance on whether a stakeholder pension is suitable for you. The guidance falls short of advice.

Several providers let you apply for stakeholder pensions online through their web sites. They include: Eagle Star Direct (*www.eaglestardirect.co.uk*), Legal & General (*www.landg.com*), Norwich Union (*norwich-union.co.uk*) and Prudential (*www.prudential.co.uk*). Typically, you then receive by post the full product information and a copy of your application to check, sign and return with your initial investment. If you intend to make regular contributions, you can usually set up a direct debit mandate online.

## Buying through an intermediary

A few intermediaries operate web sites that let you select from a range of pension providers and start your application rolling online. For example:

- Hargreaves Lansdown (*www.hlpensions.co.uk*) offers a database of stakeholder pensions and has arranged special deals for its customers with some of the providers. You cannot apply online but you can complete an online order form for further information
- Discount Pensions (*www.discountpensions.co.uk*) – the web site of consulting actuaries Geoffrey Bernstein – offers cut-price personal pensions (but not stakeholder schemes) from a panel of providers. You fill out an online form for a quote and the relevant paperwork is sent to you by post
- Tendirect (*www.10direct.com*) offers commission-free stakeholder pensions and other products in return for an annual subscription (£50 in July 2001).

Several providers offer online self-invested personal pensions (SIPPs) – tax-efficient pension wrappers into which you put the investments of your choice which can be, say, unit trusts, OEICs, investments trusts or shares. They include Sippdeal (*www.sippdeal.co.uk*) and a few stockbrokers (see page 136).

## Approaching retirement

If you are close to retirement, you might want to check out how much pension you can expect to buy with the fund you have built up. To do this check out the following IFAs that specialise in annuity business: The Annuity Bureau (*www.annuity-bureau.co.uk*) and Annuity Direct (*www. annuitydirect.co.uk*). The Annuity Bureau's web site includes excellent background information on the various annuity options and the alternative, income drawdown.

# Shares online

**8**

About 12 million people in Britain own shares. However, only 1 million or so hold what might be termed a portfolio and trade regularly. The rest tend to have just a few holdings they have picked up through privatisation issues and building society conversions, or shares received through an employee scheme at work. A survey for Proshare (*www.proshare.org.uk*) in 2000 found that two-thirds of shareholders have shares in five or fewer companies. Of these, about half have only one or two different shareholdings.

Some 305,000 share-owners have opened Internet accounts. The main advantage cited by respondents in the Proshare survey is the speed and efficiency offered by the Internet. Even if you are currently less than active as a share-owner, one day you may want to sell your shares, and the easiest and cheapest route is likely to be via the Net. If you are an active trader, the Internet also gives you the advantage of access to a vast range of data and analysis – much of which, just a few years ago, was available only to the professionals.

## The dangers of Internet trading

The Internet is not all good news for share investors. All the online broking services so far are execution-only – in other words, you do not benefit from advice. Whereas once your broker might have cautioned against your latest hare-brained scheme, the Internet gives you the freedom to indulge your whims to the full. So it is all the more important that you take the time to learn about shares, your financial goals, and how the two can marry up.

Statistics show that shareholders who trade online tend to trade more often than offline shareholders. For example, the

Proshare survey found that only about a quarter of all offline shareholders had bought shares three times or more in the 12 months before being questioned. The equivalent proportion for online traders was over three-quarters. Data from the Association of Private Client Investment Managers and Stockbrokers (*www.apcims.co.uk*) shows that, while online traders amount to only some 2.5 per cent of share-owners, they account for 29 per cent of all execution-only trades. Each time you deal, you incur commission charges; each time you buy UK shares, you pay stamp duty. So the more you deal, the greater the return you need to make to cover the costs, let alone make a profit. This is one reason why daytraders (see page 140) are very unlikely to make sustainable profits.

While there is a lot of information out there on the Net, the quality varies. Bottom of the pile has to be gossip from chatrooms and bulletin boards. You might pick up a valuable tip from these sources, but it is impossible to know whether the information has substance unless you make your own rigorous checks. Worryingly, one in six of the online traders in the Proshare survey thought bulletin boards were a reliable source of information. Never take chat at face value. Chatrooms and bulletin boards are, from time to time, hijacked by unscrupulous people running scams. The most popular is 'pump and dump'. This is where someone buys some duff shares cheaply, then spreads rumours on the Net that the company is about to strike gold. Naïve investors pile in, pushing up the share price, at which point the perpetrator of the scam sells the shares at a fat profit and leaves everyone else to get their fingers burnt.

Another ruse is to circulate damaging information about a company – even faking press releases – in order to drive down the price. The perpetrator buys the stock cheaply and then sells for a profit when the company refutes the false information and the share price recovers.

Similarly, be very wary of emails claiming to offer you exclusive information or opportunities bound to make you a fortune. Always keep in mind the golden rule: if it sounds too good to be true, it probably is.

# Shares and your financial goals

Shares are 'risk investments'. Unlike a deposit in a bank or building society, the value of shares you own can fall as well as rise, so you could lose some, or even all, of the money you invest. Shares are not the home for money that you might need back at short notice or on a set date, when share prices might be in the doldrums.

However, over the medium to long term, shares have consistently tended to outperform safer investments, and by a wide margin. For example, over the last ten years £1,000 invested in a building society account might have grown to, say, £1,370 if you had reinvested all the interest. Over the same time, £1,000 invested in shares could have grown to £3,170. So, particularly if you are investing for long-term goals – such as retirement or paying for your youngsters to go to university – investing in shares makes sense.

Investing in the shares of just one or two companies is a risky strategy, because a dip in the share price will affect a large slice of your capital. To reduce risk, you need to spread your money across a broad range of different shares. A well-balanced portfolio is likely to hold at least ten carefully chosen and diverse companies, and usually many more. However, dealing charges make it expensive to buy and sell small quantities of shares. To build up your own diverse portfolio, you should be prepared to invest at least £15,000 and ideally £50,000 or more. And that's on top of your other saving and investing – for example, to provide an emergency fund and save for shorter-term goals such as holidays and cars.

An alternative way to invest in shares is to pool together with lots of other investors and buy into a ready-made portfolio, in other words an investment fund. This is what you do when you buy unit trusts, open-ended investment companies (OEICs), investment trusts and exchange-traded funds (ETFs). Opting for an investment fund rather than direct investment in shares makes sense if:

- you have a relatively small sum to invest
- you don't want the bother of running your own share portfolio.

See Chapter 7 for guidance on investing in funds online.

There is another and quite different way to use shares. Creating or buying into a well-balanced portfolio is all about managing risk. But you might want deliberately to court risk in the hope of making exceptional profits. Stock-picking is the art of spotting shares that you reckon the market has wrongly priced and which are due for a significant rise in the near future. If your hunch is right, you can make big gains; if you get it wrong, you have incurred dealing costs for nothing; and if you get it badly wrong you may lose your money completely. Speculating in this way is closer to gambling than investing – similar to backing horses based on your judgment about their form. It can be great fun, but you should never use money that you cannot afford to lose.

## Background information

If you are new to share-owning or relatively inexperienced, it pays to do some homework before you sign up with a stock-broker (whether on- or offline). You could start with a good old-fashioned book. There are many introductory texts, including *The Which? Guide to Shares* from Which? Books.\* To deepen your understanding, you will need to move on to more specialist books that cover, say, charting and fundamental analysis. Try browsing through the bookshops available at Proshare (*www.proshare.org.uk*), Charles Schwab (*www.schwab-worldwide.com/europe*) or MoneyGuru (*www.moneyguru.co.uk*).

Proshare is an organisation that exists to promote wider share ownership. You'll find a lot of good introductory material on its site, including information about employee share schemes and starting and running an investment club. Other sources if you're just getting started are the Share Aware section of the London Stock Exchange web site (*www.london-*

*stockexchange.com*) and the FAQ section of the APCIMS site (*www.apcims.co.uk*). Some of the general personal finance web sites contain excellent introductory material on share owning and dealing – see in particular Interactive Investor (*www.iii.co.uk*), FTYourMoney (*www.ftyourmoney.com*) and Mottley Fool (*www.fool.co.uk*). Some broker sites have comprehensive guides to get you started – for example E*Trade (*www.etrade.co.uk*) and Stock Academy (*www.stock academy.com*).

If you decide to branch out into options and futures, go back to the bookshops for a general grounding and visit the London International Financial Futures and Traded Options Exchange (LIFFE) at *www.liffe.com*

## Choosing an online broker

The number of online broking firms available to UK investors has escalated rapidly over the last year or so. This chapter highlights a few, and the table below provides a fuller (but not comprehensive) list.

Which broker would suit you depends mainly on the shares you want to deal in, the pattern of your trading and the degree of extra materials and support you want onsite.

You can find lists of brokers at the London Stock Exchange and APCIMS sites (*wwwlondonstockexchange.com* and *www.apcims.co.uk*). For online help choosing a broker, try the following sites:

- **Gomez (*www.gomez.com*)** This a web site ratings service. The overall scores are heavily weighted by site content, but there are separate scores for features such as ease of use and cost. As well as ranking the online brokers, Gomez also provides thumbnail reviews of each site
- **BlueSky (*www.blueskyratings.com*)** As the name suggests, this is also a web site ratings service. The overall scores again tend to lean heavily towards site content. Although there is some breakdown by other features (for example usability), Blue Sky is not as easy to use as Gomez and does not cover as many brokers

- **MoneySupermarket** (*www.moneysupermarket.com*)
  This financial products comparison and sales web site can
  search a database of a hundred different dealing services.
  You are invited to give information about how often you
  deal on average and the average size of your deals. You
  then receive a very comprehensive listing of the broking
  services ranked by the cost of a year's trading based on the
  information you supplied.

## Online stockbrokers

| Broker | Web site | Low minimum dealing (£12 or less) | Flat-rate dealing charge | Regular charge (e.g. annual) |
| --- | --- | --- | --- | --- |
| Alliance & Leicester | www.alliance-leicester.co.uk | Y | N | Y |
| Barclays | www.barclays-stockbrokers.co.uk | Y | N | Y |
| Charles Schwab | www.schwab-worldwide.com/europe | Y | N | Y |
| Comdirect | www.comdirect.com | N | N | Y |
| DLJ Direct | www.dljdirect.co.uk | N | N | N |
| e-Cortal | www.e-cortal.com | Y | N | Y |
| Egg | www.egg.com | Y | Y | Y |
| E*Trade | www.etrade.co.uk | N[1] | Y | Y |
| Fastrade | www.fastrade.co.uk | N | N[2] | Y |
| Halifax | www.sharexpress.co.uk | N | N[2] | N |
| Hargreaves Lansdown | www.h-l.co.uk | Y | Y | Y |
| Hoodless Brennan | www.hoodlessbrennan.co.uk | N | N | Y[3] |
| iDealing | www.idealing.com | Y | Y | Y |
| IMIWeb | www.imiweb.co.uk | Y | Y | N |
| Killik & Co | www.killik.co.uk | N | N | N |
| myBroker | www.mybroker.co.uk | N | N[2] | N |
| NatWest | www.natweststockbrokers.co.uk | N | N | N |
| Nothing Ventured | www.nothing-ventured.com | N | N | Y |
| Selftrade | www.selftrade.co.uk | N | Y | N |
| The Share Centre | www.share.com | Y | N | Y |
| Sharepeople | www.sharepeople.com | N | N[2] | N |
| Stock Academy | www.stockacademy.com | N | Y | N |
| Stocktrade | www.stocktrade.co.uk | N | N | Y |
| T D Waterhouse | www.tdwaterhouse.co.uk | Y | N | N |
| Virginmoney | www.virginmoney.co.uk | N | Y | N |
| Xest | www.xest.com | N | Y | Y |

1. But 'Y' if you are a frequent trader. All traders get first 30 days' free dealing.
2. But commission rises in just two or three flat-rate steps.
3. Waived for the first year.

## The shares you want to deal in

The vast majority of UK share-owners hold and trade in large UK companies. All the online brokers cover these. However, if you want to deal in smaller companies, particularly stocks quoted on the Alternative Investment Market (AIM), check the coverage carefully before you sign up. For example, e-Cortal covers only FTSE 350 shares, and several brokers do not deal in shares (called 'residuals') that can't be settled through Crest (an electronic settlement system), including some AIM shares.

You need to select the service carefully if you want to trade in foreign shares. The London Stock Exchange had, at the time of writing, very recently started a new service called the International Retail Service (IRS), enabling UK investors to trade the shares of major European and US companies in sterling on the London market. Some online brokers include IRS dealing in their UK coverage and others are likely to follow suit. For a wider choice of foreign shares, choose, for example, e-Cortal (*www.e-cortal.co.uk*), IMIWeb (*www.imiweb.co.uk*), myBroker (*www.mybroker.co.uk*) or Sharepeople (*www.sharepeople.com*).

Most online brokers require you to transfer your shares to their nominee account before they will sell them, and to place any newly bought shares into the nominee account. A few will deal in shares using paper certificates, but for an extra charge. These include NatWest (*www.natweststockbrokers.co.uk*) – extra £3, Sharepeople (*www.sharepeople.com*) – extra £2.50, and Stockacademy (*www.stockacademy.com*) – extra £5.

## The pattern of your trading

If you are an inactive shareholder and simply want the facility to sell your existing holdings, avoid services that charge an annual or quarterly fee. Ideally, go for a service with a low minimum dealing charge, such as IMIWeb (*www.imiweb.co.uk*). If you have paper share certificates, you could choose a service that handles these, for example, NatWest (*www.natweststockbrokers.co.uk*), Sharepeople (*www.sharepeople.co.uk*) or Stock Academy (*www.stock academy.com*), but bear in mind you'll pay extra. The alternative is to first transfer your certificates to the broker's nominee account (which is usually free) and then make a paperless sale. If you intend to replace your shareholdings with an investment in unit trusts, OEICs or investment trusts, check with the investment fund manager whether it operates a share exchange scheme – this could work out cheaper than arranging your own share sale and separate fund purchase.

If you trade fairly small amounts, avoid high flat-rate commissions – these will eat heavily into a small deal. By the same token, if you trade large amounts, a flat-rate commission will take a relatively small bite out of your deal and is likely to be more cost effective than a percentage-rate commission. Large-deal traders should avoid percentage-rate commission scales with no maximum – for example, NatWest (*www.natwest-stockbrokers.co.uk*) and The Share Centre (*www.share.com*).

If you hold shares in more than just a few companies, beware of brokers that charge an annual or quarterly fee based on the number of shareholdings – for example Charles Schwab (*www.schwab-worldwide.com/europe*) and The Share Centre (*www.share.com*).

At the time of writing, the clear winner on cost was IMIWeb (*www.imiweb.co.uk*), with a flat-rate commission of £10 per deal and no annual or quarterly fee.

Note that if you want to transfer from one broker to another, there is usually a charge for transferring your shares out of the old broker's nominee account, although transfers in are free. The transfer out charge is often in the region of £10 (plus VAT) per shareholding.

## Extras

Most brokers' sites contain a full panoply of price charts, ratios, news, analysts' research, and so on. Particularly comprehensive sites include Comdirect (*www.comdirect.co.uk*) and E*Trade (*www.etrade.co.uk*). But much of this material is also available either free or for a fee at other sites, such as those listed in the table opposite. Taking advantage of this, a few brokers, in particular iDealing (*www.idealing.co.uk*), have chosen to focus purely on dealing, but provide links to sites for research, news and tools.

If you are an active trader, valuable services that bring extensive information together on to a single screen include Power E*Trade (*www.etrade.co.uk*), myBroker (*www.mybroker.co.uk*) and Comdirect (*www.comdirect.co.uk*).

## Web sites offering stock market, company and/or share information

| | |
|---|---|
| www.advfn.com | www.moneyguru.co.uk |
| www.analystinsite.co.uk | www.multexinvestor.co.uk |
| www.bloomberg.co.uk | www.newsnow.co.uk |
| www.breakingviews.com | www.news-review.co.uk |
| www.citywire.co.uk | www.proquote.net |
| www.digital-look.co.uk | www.redskyresearch.com |
| www.ft.com | www.riskgrades.com |
| www.ftmarketwatch.com | www.sharecast.com |
| www.getrealtime.com | www.sharepages.com |
| www.hemscott.net | www.stockpoint.com |
| www.iii.co.uk | www.uk-invest.com |
| www.marketeye.com | www.updata.co.uk |

## ISAs and SIPPs

About half of the online brokers allow you to operate your share-dealing through an individual savings account (ISA). The advantage of this is that the ISA manager can, until 5 April 2004, reclaim the 10 per cent tax credit on any dividends and add this to your account. Any capital gains are tax-free, and you do not have to declare any ISA investments on your tax return. However, check carefully whether there are extra charges for running the ISA account and whether these will outweigh the tax you save. Bear in mind that, as well as being able to deduct various allowances and reliefs when working out capital gains, you can make up to £7,500 (in 2001–2) in gains without paying tax anyway, so an ISA will not necessarily save you much. To find out more about ISAs, visit the Inland Revenue* web site (*www.inlandrevenue.gov.uk*) or see *Which Way to Save and Invest* from Which? Books.

A few online brokers let you trade within a self-invested personal pension (SIPP). These include Charles Schwab (*www.schwab-worldwide.com/europe*), DLJDirect (*www.dljdirect.*

*co.uk*) and Killik (*www.killik.co.uk*). With a SIPP, you get all the normal tax advantages of a pension scheme:

- full income-tax relief on the amount you invest
- tax-free gains
- some income, but not income from shares, is tax free
- you can take part of the proceeds as a tax-free lump sum.

Once again, you need to check that the tax advantages will outweigh any extra charges you incur. For more information about pensions, see *The Which? Guide to Pensions* from Which? Books.

## Getting started

Signing up with an online broker can be instant or it can take several days. The usual steps involved are:

- you fill in an application form
- you open a dealing account with the broker, into which you pay money by debit card, cheque, automated transfer (BACS) or direct debit
- you may want to transfer shares to the broker's nominee account – the broker will provide transfer forms allowing you to do this
- the broker may check your credit references, sometimes instantly, using an online search.

Where the broker lets you file the application form online and open the account using a debit card, you can usually start buying within minutes. Brokers fitting this bill include IMIWeb (*www.imiweb.co.uk*), DLJDirect (*www.dljdirect.co.uk*) and Stock Academy (*www.stockacademy.com*).

There was a time when online brokers divided into two camps: those that provided you with direct-dealing facilities (called 'straight-through dealing'), enabling you to trade immediately at the prices you see on your screen; and those that simply operated a glorified email system, passing your order to a broker who might or might not process your deal straightaway. Nowadays, virtually all online broking services offer straight-through dealing.

Many online brokers are offshoots of overseas companies. However, apart from e-Cortal, which is authorised by the French authorities, all the brokers mentioned in this chapter have set up UK operations regulated by the Financial Services Authority (FSA)* – see Chapter 2 for a discussion of the protection this gives you.

It is essential that you can still deal even if there are problems with the broker's web site or your connection to it. Nearly all online brokers also have a phone-dealing facility. With some, you simply choose whichever method of dealing you prefer; others charge you extra if you resort to the phone, unless there are problems with the broker's web site. iDealing is unusual in that it has no phone-dealing backup at all, and all contact with the broker is by online trading or email. If there are problems with the main iDealing web site, it has a second web site ready to take over. This is fine in the case of broker problems, but does not help if you are unable to deal online because of difficulties with your own computer or ISP (though you can access the service from another computer).

One of the great advantages of Internet share-dealing is that you can place your orders at any time of day or night. If the relevant stock market is open, you view the real-time price and decide whether to deal there and then. However, if the market is closed, nearly all online brokers let you leave an order on the system to be carried out the next trading day. There are two ways in which this order might be carried out:

- **at best** – the broker will deal for you, getting the highest available price if you are a seller or paying the lowest available price if you are a buyer
- **limit order** – you specify a price above which you are not willing to buy or below which you are not willing to sell.

Not all online services accept limit orders. Among those that do, many online services operate them only on a 'fill or kill' basis – this means that if your instructions can be carried out as soon as the market opens, your order is fulfilled. If not (because the available buying price is too high or the selling price too low according to your limit), the order is cancelled. A few services allow your order to stay in place for a while – for example, a 'good for the day' limit order is fulfilled at any time during the trading day that the share price comes within the limit you specified, but is cancelled if that situation has not come about by the end of the day.

## Specialist types of share-dealing

### New issues

You may be interested in buying the newly issued shares of companies coming to the stock market for the first time (called initial public offerings – IPOs). The problem is finding out what is on offer and how to get a piece of the action. Many IPOs are placed direct with institutions – pension funds and other fund managers – bypassing private investors altogether.

Fortunately, there are a number of web sites that carry information about new issues coming up. They include the London Stock Exchange (*www.londonstockexchange.com*) and Interactive Investor (*www.iii.co.uk/newissues*). However, if you are keen to invest, your best bet is to register with a specialist, such as EO (*www.eo.net*). EO is a European company that, by building links with investment banks and venture capital firms, is able to offer newly issued shares to private investors. Instead of registering direct with EO, you can access the EO service through participating stockbrokers – which, at the time of writing, were as shown in the table below.

**Online brokers offering access to new issues**[1]

| Broker | Web site |
| --- | --- |
| Barclays | *www.barclaysstockbrokers.co.uk* |
| Charles Schwab | *www.schwab-worldwide/europe* |
| IMIWeb | *www.imiweb.co.uk* |
| Sharepeople | *www.sharepeople.com* |
| Stock Academy | *www.stockacademy.com* |
| Stocktrade | *www.stocktrade.co.uk* |

1. Through links to EO as at July 2001.

## Daytrading

Daytrading (also called 'direct access trading') is the practice of actively buying and selling shares over a very short time horizon in order to make a profit from even very small differences in prices and spreads. It has little to do with the fundamentals behind the value of a share and more to do with exploiting imperfections in the market.

Shares are usually quoted at two prices – a higher offer price at which you can buy, and a lower bid price at which you can sell. The difference (the 'spread') between the two prices is the reward to the market-makers – the professionals committed to buying and selling in order to ensure there is a ready market in shares. A daytrader is, in effect, aiming to act like a market-maker and buy in shares at the bid price to sell on at the higher offer price. Daytraders also compare the spreads of different market-makers, watching for discrepancies that open up opportunities to buy cheap and sell at a higher price (a form of arbitrage sometimes called 'scalping'), and use a variety of other techniques.

Daytrading requires a large pool of capital and specialist software. You need a lot of capital because you are trying to profit from small price differences, but each deal will incur commission and, in the UK, stamp duty. Suppose, for example, that you can buy a company's shares at 675p and sell immediately at 680p. If you could afford only 1,000 shares, you would pay £6,750 plus, say, £9 commission and 0.5 per cent stamp duty, which comes to £33.75. You would resell at £6800 less £9 commission, leaving you with a net loss of £1.75. If you could trade 10,000 shares, you would instead make a net profit of £144.50. And, if you could avoid paying stamp duty – as you would if you were buying on a US stock market – you could boost your profit to £482 (ignoring currency conversion costs).

From the brief description above, it is clear that the average online broking service does not give you the detailed information you need to spot and exploit discrepancies in the market. You need to use software that shows you all the bids and offers available in the market at any time and the volumes being traded. This so-called 'Level II' information has, until

139

recently, been available only for US markets, though it is now being made available for the largest shares traded on the London Stock Exchange.

Daytrading is better established in the US than the UK. Research by the US Securities and Exchange Commission (SEC) estimated that 70 per cent of US daytraders lose money. Making profits is even harder in the UK because of the hefty impact of stamp duty on purchases. However, if the idea still appeals, take a look at *www.directaccesstrader.com*

## Comdirect
## www.comdirect.co.uk

SHARES YOU CAN DEAL IN: Most UK, US and European shares.
COST: £5 commission on sales up to £500. £12.50 flat commission on other deals up to £5,000. £14.50 on deals over £5,000. Extra fee of £5 for telephone orders. Annual fee: £25. (£7.50 commission per deal and no annual fee for investment clubs.) £10 charge if you require paper certificate. Transfers out: £10 per shareholding to a maximum of £100.
SERVICES: Limit orders and stop-loss orders accepted. You can hold your shares in ISAs and personal equity plans (PEPs). Download or order company reports and accounts. Comprehensive market and company information (available free to all Web users and not just Comdirect customers). Watchlists and portfolio monitoring and tracking.

## DLJ Direct
## www.dljdirect.co.uk

SHARES YOU CAN DEAL IN: UK, international shares quoted on the London Stock Exchange's International Retail Service, and US.
COST: £14.95 commission on deals up to £1,500. £19.95 flat commission on larger deals. No annual fee. Transfers out: £15 per shareholding.
SERVICES: Limit orders, but only on a fill or kill basis. You can hold shares through ISAs, PEPs or SIPPs. Comprehensive onsite research and market and company information.

## e-Cortal
**www.e-cortal.com**

SHARES YOU CAN DEAL IN: London (FTSE 350 and AIM), New York, NASDAQ, Frankfurt, Paris, Zurich, Madrid, Amsterdam and Milan.

COST: €15 (approximately £10) commission for deals up to €5,000 (around £2,985) and 0.3 per cent for larger transactions. €5 (approximately £20) for limit orders up to €5,000.

Services: Limit orders. Investment research provided by BNP Paribas.

## E*Trade
**www.etrade.co.uk**

SHARES YOU CAN DEAL IN: UK, international shares quoted on the London Stock Exchange International Retail Service, and US.

COST: £14.95 commission for first 30 trades a quarter (except deals over £1,500, which are £19.95). Flat-rate £8.95 per deal if you trade more than 30 times a quarter. £29.95 per deal if you trade by phone. £4.85 per month account management fee. Transfers out: £15 + VAT per shareholding. Research is free for traders or £5 + VAT per month for non-traders.

SERVICES: Limit orders on fill or kill basis. You can hold shares through ISAs. Comprehensive research, market information and quotes. Stock-selection tools provided by DigitalLook. Knowledge centre especially helpful if you are new to investing. Power E*Trade service provides greater depth of information for active traders.

## Hargreaves Lansdown
**www.h-l.co.uk**

SHARES YOU CAN DEAL IN: UK, including AIM.

COST: £9.95 flat commission per trade. Phone dealing costs 1 per cent on deals up to £10,000, with a minimum of £15. £12.50 + VAT per quarter account management fee. Transfers out: £12.50 per shareholding.

SERVICES: Limit orders on fill or kill basis. Market and company information, research and newsletters.

## iDealing
### www.idealing.co.uk

SHARES YOU CAN DEAL IN: UK (except residual shares).

COST: Flat charge of £10 per trade. Administration fee of £5 per quarter. Transfers out: £15 per shareholding. Transfers in: free unless paper certificates, which are charged at £5 per holding.

SERVICES: Limit order facility available on request. You can hold shares through ISAs and PEPs. No research, news or charts, but links to recommended sites that provide these. No backup phone dealing, but complete backup web site in case of problems.

## IMIWeb
### www.imiweb.co.uk

SHARES YOU CAN DEAL IN: You can use a single sterling account to trade shares on the following stock exchanges: London, New York, Frankfurt, Paris, Milan, Amsterdam and Brussels.

COST: £10 flat charge per deal for UK stocks; £15 flat charge per deal for international stocks. Extra £10 + VAT if you require a paper certificate. £10 + VAT per shareholding if you transfer out to another broker.

SERVICES: New issues service.

## myBroker
### www.mybroker.co.uk

SHARES YOU CAN DEAL IN: UK and US.

COST: £12.50 per trade on deals up to £2,500, £25 on larger deals. No administration fee. $15 (or £ equivalent) charge for live-feed prices in any calendar month that you do not deal.

SERVICES: Limit orders. News, market and company data. Traded options service.

## Charles Schwab
### www.schwab-worldwide.com/europe

SHARES YOU CAN DEAL IN: UK (but not residual shares) and US. (You need a separate dollar account to trade in US shares.)

COST: £12 commission for trades up to £1,000. £15 on deals from £1,001 to £2,000, £24 on deals from £2,001 to £4,000, rising in further steps to a maximum of £50 on deals over £20,000. (Higher rates for deals by phone.) Administration charge: £1 per holding per quarter (minimum £5, maximum £30). Transfers out: £10 per holding (minimum £30). Different charges for frequent traders.

SERVICES: Limit orders. You can hold shares in ISAs and SIPPs. Market and company news and research, charts, comprehensive background information and bookshop. New issues service.

## Sharepeople
### www.sharepeople.com

SHARES YOU CAN DEAL IN: UK, US and Europe.
Cost: £14.50 commission on UK deals up to £1,000; £17.50 on larger UK deals and all non-UK trades. Extra £2.50 for deals involving paper certificates. Nominee account charges of £1 per holding per quarter. Transfers out: £10 per holding.
SERVICES: News and education centre. New issues service.

## Stock Academy
### www.stockacademy.com

SHARES YOU CAN DEAL IN: UK (but not residual shares).
Cost: £15 flat-rate fee per trade. Extra £5 for deals including paper certificates. No annual or quarterly fee. Transfers out: £10 + VAT per shareholding.
SERVICES: Limit orders – both fill or kill and good for the day. General and share news, information supplied by UKiNvest. New issues service.

## T D Waterhouse
### www.tdwaterhouse.co.uk

SHARES YOU CAN DEAL IN: UK, US and Europe.
Cost: £9.75 on deals up to £500, £12.50 on deals from £501 to £1,501, and increasing scale to a maximum of £24.95 on deals over £4,000. Lower rates available for frequent traders (25 or more deals a year). You pay extra if you deal by phone. No administration charge. Transfers out: £10 per shareholding.
SERVICES: You can hold shares through ISAs and PEPs. News and data services.

# Mortgages online

# 9

There are an estimated 4,900 different mortgages on offer in the UK, and around 140 lenders. Checking the whole market to make sure you get the best deal can be a daunting task. In fact, surveys suggest that most people do not even attempt it. Taking out a mortgage is generally split into two stages: getting an overview of what's available and shopping around for a specific product. The table below shows where people go to get an overview.

**Where people start to get information about mortgages**

| Source | Percentage of respondents using this source |
| --- | --- |
| Look at branches on the high street | 32% |
| Go to existing lender | 15% |
| Contact a financial adviser/intermediary | 11% |
| Ask friends/family | 3% |
| Read best-buy tables in the press | 1% |
| Look in national newspapers | 1% |
| Look in specialist mortgage/homeowners' press | 1% |
| Use the Internet | 1% |
| Go to a specified outlet bank/building society | 7% |
| Other | 1% |
| Not applicable/don't know/not stated | 26% |

*Source*: Council of Mortgage Lenders, 1999.

When it comes to the shopping-around stage, recent research by the Financial Services Authority (FSA)* reported that only about half of all consumers shop around at all. One survey found that 10 per cent of borrowers look at two lenders, 21 per cent consider three, and only 11 per cent look at four or more lenders. Another 11 per cent went to a financial adviser or other intermediary (such as a mortgage broker) at the first stage. The adviser would normally then handle the second stage and shop around for the borrower among a range of lenders, in some cases drawn from the whole market.

So far, the Internet has not figured greatly in the hunt for mortgages, but its popularity is likely to grow as it is an ideal medium for rapidly sifting through the thousands of mortgages on offer. The Internet can also contribute to the process in other ways – see below.

## Background information

When you first set out to find a mortgage, you might have only the haziest notion of what sort of products are out there and which would be suitable for you. This is especially so if you are a first-time buyer, but surveys show that even among experienced homebuyers and people seeking to remortgage, around a quarter lack the basic information they need.

Most web sites that compare or sell mortgages have some introductory material, usually a guide to home-buying or remortgaging, and often a jargon-busting glossary. Not surprisingly, if you go to a lender's own site, the material tends to be oriented towards its own products. More impartial and comprehensive guides are available from product-comparison sites such as MoneyeXtra (*www.moneyextra.com*), Interactive Investor (*www.iii.co.uk*) and FT Your Money (*www.ftyourmoney.com*).

Another good source of impartial guidance is the FSA web site (*www.fsa.gov.uk*). It publishes *The FSA guide to repaying your mortgage*, which can be downloaded from the site and, in its consumer section, includes FAQs about mortgages as well as a guide to shopping around. In 2002, the FSA web site is due to start publishing its own tables comparing mortgage products.

The Council of Mortgage Lenders (CML)* publishes detailed guides to buying a home (including a Scottish version) and to the different types of mortgage product. These guides can be downloaded from the CML web site (*www.cml.org.uk*).

Nearly all lenders and mortgage advisers subscribe to the Mortgage Code, which sets out standards of good practice that lenders should follow when doing business with you. You can check out the Code at the web site of the Mortgage Code Compliance Board (*www.mortgagecode.co.uk*).

For other sources of background information, *Which?* magazine regularly publishes articles about mortgages and you'll find a detailed chapter in *Be Your Own Financial Adviser* published by Which? Books. Newsagents stock specialist magazines devoted to mortgages. See the box below for a quick introduction to the main types of mortgage product.

---

## The main types of mortgage product

**Which type of loan?**

- **repayment (also called 'capital and interest')** Your monthly payments pay the interest and gradually repay the amount you borrowed. If you keep up all the payments, the loan is guaranteed to be completely paid off by the end of the mortgage term
- **interest-only** Your monthly payments pay only the interest. Usually, you simultaneously pay into an investment that builds up a lump sum you use at the end of the term to pay off the loan. If the investment is an endowment policy, you are said to have an 'endowment mortgage'. With an 'ISA mortgage', you invest in an ISA (usually a stocks and shares ISA). You need to review the investment regularly to check it is still on track to repay the loan

**Which type of interest?**

- **variable rate** A mortgage rate that goes up and down broadly in line with changes in interest rates in the economy as a whole
- **standard variable rate (SVR)** The variable rate of interest a lender charges on its basic mortgages

---

- **base-rate tracker** A variable rate that is linked to some specific interest rate, such as the Bank of England's base rate, the rate at which banks lend to each other (LIBOR) or the lender's own base rate. Each rise or fall in the specified rate causes the mortgage rate to rise or fall by exactly the same amount
- **discounted variable rate** A variable rate that is guaranteed to be a set amount lower than the lender's SVR. For example, if the SVR is 7 per cent and the discount is 2 per cent, the discounted rate will be 5 per cent. If the SVR rises to 8 per cent, the discounted rate becomes 6 per cent, and so on. Discounted rates are usually offered for a short period only, for example the first year or two
- **fixed rate** An interest rate that stays at a set level regardless of any movement in interest rates in the economy as a whole. Usually fixed rates are offered for a set period of time (say, one to ten years) and there is normally a penalty if you pay off or switch the mortgage during that period. The advantage of fixed rates is that your mortgage payments are constant, so you can budget with certainty
- **capped rate** A variable rate of interest, but one that is guaranteed not to rise above a set level, even if general interest rates carry on rising. Capped rates are usually offered for a set period of time, for example the first one to ten years. The advantage of a capped rate is that you know your mortgage payments will not exceed a given ceiling, helping you to budget
- **collared rate** A variable rate that will not, however, fall below a set level even if general interest rates carry on falling. You might have to accept a collared rate in order to qualify for a special deal.

**Other variations**

- **flexible mortgage** You can choose to vary your monthly payments. Making overpayments lets you pay off your mortgage faster. Underpayments or payment holidays may be useful if your finances are temporarily stretched

- **current account mortgage (CAM)** Your current account, mortgage and sometimes other savings accounts and loans are linked (see page 60). Money in the current account (and any savings accounts) is set off against your mortgage loan (and any other loans), reducing the outstanding balance and so the interest charged
- **CAT-standard mortgage** A loan that meets certain conditions designed to give you value for money. For example, a variable rate CAT standard mortgage must be a base-rate tracker and have no redemption charges if you pay off part or all of the loan before the end of the mortgage term – a handy benchmark against which to compare other loans
- **cashback** A cash lump sum you receive when your mortgage advance is paid. The cash can be used in any way you like. Usually available only with SVR loans
- **buy-to-let** A mortgage used to buy a property that you intend to rent out to other people
- **self-certification** A loan made on the basis of the income you have declared but for which you have provided no proof of earnings. Because the lender has to rely on your word, and is therefore taking on extra risk, you are charged a higher-than-normal interest rate
- **sub-prime** Loan made to someone with a poor credit history. Because the lender is taking on extra risk of not getting its money back, a higher-than-normal interest rate is charged.

## Calculators

Nearly all mortgage web sites offer a variety of calculators to help you make your mortgage decisions. The most common calculators you'll find are described below.

Note that, although calculators do ask for some sensitive information, such as how much you earn or want to borrow, most do not operate over a secure site. Provided you have not also been asked for personal details (name, address, and so on), this should not be a cause for concern. Simple calculators do not store the information you give, and you are free to key in any figures you like.

## How much can you borrow?

The maximum you can borrow (subject to satisfactory credit checks and property valuation) is a multiple of your income. Common multiples are:

- three times your own before-tax income plus the income of your partner, if you have one, or
- two-and-a-half times the joint income of you and your partner.

However, some lenders are willing to give you more, for example four times your income. Most calculators reduce your income for any regular credit-card or loan commitments you have before working out the maximum mortgage you can get.

If you are visiting the web site of a lender, the calculator will reflect that lender's own income multiples. If you are using the web site of a product-comparison site (see page 154), the calculator might generate a list of different lenders and varying maximum loans reflecting the lending policies of each.

## How much can you afford to borrow?

This will be some type of budgeting calculator where you key in details of your monthly income and your main expenses. The calculator works out the surplus of your income over your spending and this is the amount you can afford to pay each month for your mortgage. The better calculators then use this monthly payment to work out the size of loan you can afford on either a repayment or interest-only basis.

Some calculators ask for a lot of detail about your spending, which can be tedious to input but produces a more accurate result; others take a broad-brush approach.

## How much will a mortgage cost me?

The third common calculator works out how much you would have to pay each month for a mortgage of a given size at a particular interest rate and paid off over a given term. The

**How much can you borrow?**

Single borrower ●
Two borrowers ○

Your total annual income (before tax)

First borrower     £ `38000`

Second borrower    £ `            `

Total              £ `38000`

**Your monthly credit commitments**

First borrower     £ `230`

Second borrower    £ `            `

Total              £ `230`

**Your annual disposal income**

                   £ `35240`

[ Calculate ]    [ Reset ]

**The amount you can borrow**

                   £ `114530`

exact calculation varies slightly from one lender to another and one calculator to another, depending on assumptions made. But the answers should be broadly in line with the amounts shown in the table below.

**How much can you afford to borrow?**

Total monthly income     £ 2600

Total monthly expenses     £ 1970

Your available income each month     £ 630

You can afford a mortgage of this amount*:

Repayment     £ 90100

Interest-only**     £ 111900

\* assuming 25-year term and current standard variable rates
\*\* excluding any allowances for payments to an investment product to pay off the loan

## Special deals on the Net

Chapter 6 looked at savings accounts and found a respectable selection of Internet-only accounts, mainly offering high interest rates, reflecting in part strong competition but also the reduced overheads and administration costs of operating accounts online. You might expect to find the same factors at work in the home-loan market, but in fact special Internet mortgage deals are rare.

The few lenders offering a special Internet-only product in July 2001 are listed in the table on page 153. Other lenders have dabbled in the past but have withdrawn their Internet offerings. Two possible reasons have been suggested for the lack of cheap Internet-only deals. First, the bulk of the cost for a lender offering a mortgage is the cost of raising the money (either from savers or from wholesale money markets). As a result, any savings in administration by selling online rather than through branches or by phone have only a slight impact on the overall cost of the loan. Second, while

## Monthly cost of each £1,000 you borrow[1]

| Interest rate % | Repayment mortgage if the term is: | | | | Interest-only mortgage[2] |
|---|---|---|---|---|---|
| | 10 years | 15 years | 20 years | 25 years | |
| 2.00% | £9.19 | £6.43 | £5.05 | £4.23 | £1.67 |
| 2.25% | £9.30 | £6.54 | £5.17 | £4.35 | £1.88 |
| 2.50% | £9.41 | £6.65 | £5.29 | £4.47 | £2.08 |
| 2.75% | £9.53 | £6.77 | £5.40 | £4.60 | £2.29 |
| 3.00% | £9.64 | £6.89 | £5.53 | £4.72 | £2.50 |
| 3.25% | £9.75 | £7.00 | £5.65 | £4.85 | £2.71 |
| 3.50% | £9.86 | £7.12 | £5.77 | £4.98 | £2.92 |
| 3.75% | £9.98 | £7.24 | £5.90 | £5.11 | £3.13 |
| 4.00% | £10.09 | £7.36 | £6.02 | £5.24 | £3.33 |
| 4.25% | £10.21 | £7.48 | £6.15 | £5.37 | £3.54 |
| 4.50% | £10.32 | £7.60 | £6.28 | £5.51 | £3.75 |
| 4.75% | £10.44 | £7.73 | £6.41 | £5.64 | £3.96 |
| 5.00% | £10.55 | £7.85 | £6.54 | £5.78 | £4.17 |
| 5.25% | £10.67 | £7.97 | £6.67 | £5.92 | £4.38 |
| 5.50% | £10.79 | £8.10 | £6.80 | £6.06 | £4.58 |
| 5.75% | £10.90 | £8.23 | £6.94 | £6.20 | £4.79 |
| 6.00% | £11.02 | £8.35 | £7.07 | £6.35 | £5.00 |
| 6.25% | £11.14 | £8.48 | £7.21 | £6.49 | £5.21 |
| 6.50% | £11.26 | £8.61 | £7.35 | £6.64 | £5.42 |
| 6.75% | £11.38 | £8.74 | £7.49 | £6.78 | £5.63 |
| 7.00% | £11.50 | £8.87 | £7.62 | £6.93 | £5.83 |
| 7.25% | £11.62 | £9.00 | £7.76 | £7.08 | £6.04 |
| 7.50% | £11.74 | £9.13 | £7.91 | £7.23 | £6.25 |
| 7.75% | £11.86 | £9.26 | £8.05 | £7.38 | £6.46 |
| 8.00% | £11.99 | £9.40 | £8.19 | £7.53 | £6.67 |
| 8.25% | £12.11 | £9.53 | £8.34 | £7.69 | £6.88 |
| 8.50% | £12.23 | £9.66 | £8.48 | £7.84 | £7.08 |
| 8.75% | £12.35 | £9.80 | £8.63 | £8.00 | £7.29 |
| 9.00% | £12.48 | £9.93 | £8.77 | £8.15 | £7.50 |
| 9.25% | £12.60 | £10.07 | £8.92 | £8.31 | £7.71 |
| 9.50% | £12.73 | £10.21 | £9.07 | £8.47 | £7.92 |

1. Assumes interest is calculated monthly. If interest is worked out daily, you'll pay a bit less. If it is worked out yearly, you'll pay a bit more.
2. In addition, you will usually need to pay into an investment to build up a lump sum to repay the loan at the end of the term.

people are happy to gather mortgage information online, relatively few people go on to take out their mortgage online. National Opinion Poll (NOP) found that 17 per cent of Internet users had sought out mortgage information online but only 5 per cent took out their loan over the Web. Consumers seem to prefer a traditional service, either face-to-face in a branch or at least talking to someone at the end of a phone.

**Lenders offering special deals over the Internet in July 2001**

| Lender | Web site | Type of mortgage deal |
|---|---|---|
| Coventry Building Society | *www.remortgages.co.uk* | Fixed- and capped-rate loans aimed at existing borrowers seeking to switch lender |
| Market Harborough Building Society | *www.mhbs.co.uk* | Discounted, collared variable-rate loans |
| Norwich and Peterborough Building Society | *www.netmastergold.co.uk* | Discounted variable-rate loans, including flexible mortgages and tracker mortgages |
| West Bromwich Building Society | *www.westbrom.co.uk* | Discounted variable-rate loans (also available to non-Internet direct customers and through intermediaries) |

*Source: Moneyfacts, July 2001.*

## Online applications

It is not just the lenders in the table above that let you apply for your mortgage over the Internet. Many others – particularly the larger lenders such as Abbey National (*www.abbey national.co.uk*), Halifax (*www.halifax.co.uk*), Nationwide (*www.nationwide.co.uk*) and Woolwich (*www.woolwich.co.uk*) – offer this option, as do most of the online product-comparison services (see overleaf).

As a preliminary step, before completing a full mortgage application, some lenders can give you a very rapid 'agreement in principle'. This is an agreement (or refusal) to lend you a specified sum based on the information you have supplied about yourself and the property you want to buy. For example, Abbey National is able to provide an agreement in principle within two hours, Halifax claims to take just one minute. An agreement in principle does not mean you will definitely get the loan – this will depend on proof of your income, checking your credit references and the valuation put on the property.

Many of the web sites that let you make a full application online also have a mortgage tracking service that lets you check the progress of your mortgage application by logging on to a secure site using an identification code and password.

## Product-comparison sites

If you have not yet decided which mortgage to apply for, product-comparison sites can help you choose. These tend to be either the sites of mortgage advisers, such as John Charcol, or financial information sites, such as MoneyeXtra and Interactive Investor, which have often entered into a deal with a mortgage broker to provide online application facilities.

Typically, product-comparison sites have a large database covering some – or, in a few cases, substantially all – of the market. You can search for mortgage products that have the features you want. The sort of criteria you'll be asked to specify include:

- the purpose of the mortgage: for example first-time purchase, remortgage, moving home, buy-to-let
- the amount you want to borrow
- the value of the property
- the type of mortgage: in other words, repayment or interest-only
- the mortgage term you want
- the type of interest deal you want: variable, fixed, capped or discounted. If the latter categories, you'll be asked how long you would like the fix, cap or discount to run for

- whether you have a poor credit record – for example any county court judgements outstanding against you
- your income and whether you will be able to provide proof of it
- your employment status
- whether you want a mortgage with no upfront fees or arrangement costs
- whether you want a mortgage that does not require you to take out insurance with the lender (for example contents or buildings insurance or mortgage payment protection insurance)
- whether you want to avoid mortgages with redemption penalties or 'extended tie-ins' (in other words, redemption penalties that last beyond the period of any fixed-rate, discounted-rate or other special deal).

The precise questions and complexity of the questionnaire vary from one site to another. The more information you give, the more easily the search can be narrowed down to a shortlist of possible products. If you give little information, you may still be left with several hundred mortgages to choose from.

Some databases let you search for a mortgage based on the most competitive cost over a given time period. This draws on the fact that many mortgages are not held for the full original term. While the original term is often 25 years, the average lifetime of a mortgage is only around seven years. This type of search lets you find the mortgage likely to work out cheapest over the actual time you expect to borrow.

Most of the comparison sites let you apply for some or all of the mortgages online. In some cases there is a fee for taking out a mortgage through the site.

Some of the most popular comparison sites are looked at below. Note that this is a particularly volatile section of the Internet with a constant stream of web sites coming and going.

## CharcolOnline
**www.charcolonline.co.uk**

THE SITE: The Web-based arm of mortgage brokers John Charcol. The site includes background information, calcu-

lators and a find-a-mortgage 'wizard'. Some interesting inno-
vations, such as a 'divorcee mortgage' designed for people
relying on income from maintenance payments.

MORTGAGES AND LENDERS COVERED: Over 500 loans from 45
lenders. These include the top 20 or so lenders plus a
changing selection of other lenders selected by John Charcol.

COST IF YOU BUY ONLINE: John Charcol usually provides
mortgage advice for a fee, but if you buy online the fee is
waived. Some mortgage deals listed are exclusive to
CharcolOnline.

SUPPORT: 'Call me' button, through which you can arrange for
a mortgage adviser to phone you if you want more advice.

## Creditweb
### www.creditweb.co.uk

THE SITE: Creditweb is a European e-finance company offering
mortgage advice. The site offers two ways to search for a
mortgage: 'How much could I save by changing my mortgage?'
and 'Find the right mortgage'. Both lead to a shortlist of
products and illustrations showing how much you would pay.
The site also offers calculators and a glossary.

MORTGAGES AND LENDERS COVERED: The site covers products from
130 lenders. You can phone for information about other
products or lenders.

COST IF YOU BUY ONLINE: No direct charge. Creditweb receives
commission from mortgage lenders.

SUPPORT: 'Call me' service if you want an adviser to phone you.
Freephone helpline, Monday to Friday 9am to 8pm, Saturday
10am to 4pm.

## Fred Finds
### www.fredfinds.com

THE SITE: Web site of mortgage brokers Netwindfall, in
conjunction with Moneyquest, another firm of brokers.
Includes calculators and find-a-mortgage search. The site also
lets you track the progress of your application if you apply
through the site.

MORTGAGES AND LENDERS COVERED: Products from 11 lenders,
though you can email to find out about other products.

COST IF YOU BUY ONLINE: Information and searches are free, but Fred Finds charges a fee (typically £45) if you apply for a mortgage through the site.

SUPPORT: Freephone number for help using the site. You can also email to arrange for a mortgage adviser to phone you.

## FT Your Money
### www.ftyourmoney.com

THE SITE: Personal-finance web site owned by the Financial Times and offering a mortgage search and online application service in conjunction with Network Data and its subsidiary, The Mortgage Clearing Centre. Lots of background information, mortgage news, calculators, rates tables, glossary and 'get a mortgage' search facility.

MORTGAGES AND LENDERS COVERED: Products from 116 lenders.

COST IF YOU BUY ONLINE: No direct charge. FT Your Money and the companies it works with may receive commission from lenders.

SUPPORT: Email support only.

## Interactive Investor
### www.iii.co.uk

THE SITE: Personal-finance site, recently bought by Australian financial conglomerate AMP. Mortgage information and application services provided by John Charcol. The site provides background information, mortgage news and calculators. To search for a mortgage you transfer to CharcolOnline (see page 155).

MORTGAGES AND LENDERS COVERED: See CharcolOnline.

COST IF YOU BUY ONLINE: See CharcolOnline.

SUPPORT: See CharcolOnline.

## MoneyeXtra
### www.moneyextra.com

THE SITE: Owned by Bristol & West, MoneyeXtra was originally a financial information site but is in the process of developing comprehensive online advice as well. Almost overwhelming array of background information, news, calculators and other tools. Mortgage search lets you select mortgages according to their cost over the actual time you expect to keep the mortgage loan (rather than the original mortgage term). From the results of the search you can call up a very detailed illustration that not only summarises the particular mortgage deal but includes estimates of your overall moving costs as well.

MORTGAGES AND LENDERS COVERED: Over 4,900 products from 140 lenders.

COSTS IF YOU BUY ONLINE: No direct cost. MoneyeXtra is paid by lenders.

SUPPORT: Local-rate helpline and call-back service if you want a mortgage adviser to phone you.

## Moneyfacts
## www.moneyfacts.co.uk

THE SITE: Moneyfacts is an information specialist that constantly monitors a wide selection of personal finance markets. Its mortgage coverage is comprehensive. This is strictly a product information site – no guides or fancy tools here. You can either call up a selection of the top six products in specified categories (such as discounted products, fixed rates with no extended tie-in, and so on) or you can do a full search for products meeting the criteria you specify.

MORTGAGES AND LENDERS COVERED: The whole market.

COST IF YOU BUY ONLINE: Not applicable – you cannot apply through this site.

SUPPORT: Not applicable – Moneyfacts is purely a product information provider. (Follow 'About us' if you need to contact Moneyfacts, but be aware that it does not give mortgage advice.)

## Moneynet
## www.moneynet.co.uk

THE SITE: Personal-finance site offering a mortgage application service in conjunction with independent financial adviser Inter-Alliance. The mortgage section lets you search for mortgage products and list the results in a variety of ways. In particular, you can calculate the total cost of each mortgage over any number of years you specify (rather than simply the mortgage term).

MORTGAGES AND LENDERS COVERED: Products from over 100 lenders.

COST IF YOU BUY ONLINE: No direct cost. Moneynet may receive commission from lenders.

SUPPORT: Freephone helpline and call-back service if you want an adviser to phone you.

---

## MoneySupermarket
### www.moneysupermarket.com

THE SITE: Personal-finance shopping site letting you compare and buy a wide range of financial products. You can search for mortgage deals and in many cases apply online. The search allows you to rank deals according to their cost over a specified number of years (rather than simply the full term). MoneySupermarket is also, at the time of writing, the only UK site to offer a mortgage auction – see overleaf.

MORTGAGES AND LENDERS COVERED: Over 4,000 mortgages.

COST IF YOU BUY ONLINE: No direct charge. MoneySupermarket gets introduction fees from the lenders.

SUPPORT: Email 'Mortgage doctor' – you supply your details and the MoneySupermarket research team finds suitable mortgage products for you.

---

## UK Mortgages Online
### www.ukmortgagesonline.co.uk

THE SITE: Mortgage data and application service provided by Network Data and its subsidiary The Mortgage Clearing Centre. You can search the database for mortgages that fit the criteria you have chosen. You can also call up a list of all lenders and check out each one's products. The site also includes calculators.

MORTGAGES AND LENDERS COVERED: Over 3,500 products from 134 lenders.

COST IF YOU BUY ONLINE: No direct cost. UK Mortgages Online may receive commission from lenders.

SUPPORT: Call-back service if you want an adviser to phone you.

## *Mortgage auctions*

The web sites looked at so far let you trawl through the products on offer and make your choice accordingly – you do the hard work and passively accept whatever deals the market has to offer. MoneySupermarket (*www.moneysupermarket.com*) offers an auction service that stands the normal shopping process on its head.

You provide the usual details about yourself, the property involved and the type of mortgage you are looking for. You must also key in your bank details. Then a panel of lenders bids for your custom by offering you a deal that is guaranteed to be better than their standard off-the-shelf range of mort-gages. The best three offers are forwarded to you by email. However, this does not guarantee you the best deal on the market – other lenders may have a better product for you, and you can check this out by doing a search through the main database either on the MoneySupermarket site or another product-comparison site. The mortgage auction is restricted to people seeking to borrow £150,000 or more.

# Insurance online

# 10

Although insurance companies and brokers have, on the whole, been slow to embrace the Internet as a way of selling their products, the scale of interest has increased dramatically over the last year or so. There is now a wealth of sites offering the mainstream policies, namely car insurance, home insurance and travel cover. And an increasing number of sites are offering term insurance. A handful of Internet outlets offer other products, such as boat insurance, pet insurance and health policies.

Online insurance sites fall mainly into three categories:

- providers offering their products online
- brokers providing quotes, usually from a panel of insurers, and an online application service
- product-comparison sites – often using brokers to provide a quotation and application service.

To get an online quote, you need to complete a questionnaire. Usually these are relatively short, in which case the quote is indicative, and you may have to provide additional information if you decide to go ahead and apply online. Sometimes the questionnaire is lengthy and may seem overkill just for a quote. However, there is a trade-off: the more information you give, the more accurate the quote is likely to be.

You are typically invited to read through a list of criteria before the quote service begins. For example, in the case of travel insurance, the list will include statements that no one in your party suffers from asthma, heart problems, and so on. You proceed only if you can agree with all the statements on the list. Many online services do not cater for special cases such as these, so if you are not a standard risk, you'll probably do better dealing face-to-face or by phone with a broker who can seek out an appropriate deal. Most of the broker and product-comparison web sites include a phone number for help and more complex quotes.

To buy insurance online, you usually pay by debit card or credit card. If you intend to make regular payments, you can often set up a direct debit online. As when buying anything over the Internet, you need to take precautions:

- check that the web site includes bricks-and-mortar contact details – preferably an address as well as a phone number
- check the security policy to satisfy yourself that personal information and payment details are communicated over a secure connection and, if retained by the web site provider, stored safely behind a firewall or on another server
- check the privacy policy to see what further use, if any, may be made of your personal details.

If you are concerned about the idea of using your credit or debit card online, see Chapter 16 for ideas on protecting yourself.

Many insurance Internet sites also accept claims online. Make sure you have back-up contact details just in case you can't get online when you need to make a claim.

## Background information

For the low-down on how different types of insurance can meet your needs and what typical policies cover, a good starting point is the consumer web site of the Association of British Insurers (ABI) (*www.insurance.org.uk/consumer2/consumer.htm*). The site includes a large number of leaflets covering different types of insurance and associated matters that can all be downloaded.

For a guide to the service you should expect from insurance companies and intermediaries, refer to the General Insurance Standards Council* (*www.gisc.org.uk*).

For lists of sites relating to different types of insurance, visit Financial Information Network Directory (*www.find.co.uk/insurance*), which has sections dealing with car insurance, bike insurance, travel, life, and so on. Clicking on each name listed takes you to the relevant web site.

## Providers online

Some insurance companies now have well-developed web sites that allow you to get quotes and apply for insurance online. A selection of these is shown in the table overleaf.

Being able to get a quote and apply online can be very convenient, but going straight to a provider means you miss out on shopping around and perhaps getting a better deal elsewhere.

## Brokers and product-comparison sites

Brokers and product-comparison sites (such as MoneyeXtra and MoneySupermarket) generally select a product for you from a range of providers. The number of products and providers may be relatively small, since many brokers deal with a panel of, say, ten or so insurers. A few sites, such as MoneySupermarket, make a much wider search (over 1,000 travel policies and over 100 term insurance policies).

Do not assume that, just because a broker or product-comparison site selects from several providers for one type of insurance, that this is the case with all the insurance products it offers. For example, Egg selects car or home insurance from a panel of seven insurers, but offers a single travel insurance deal under the Egg brand.

Because most online brokers and comparison services check out only a handful of providers, you should not assume that using the Internet will necessarily throw up the cheapest or best deal. You might be wise to check out one or two traditional brokers too.

For example, the table on page 165 compares a few quotes for life cover collected online, with the deals given in the specialist magazine *Moneyfacts Life & Pensions*. Some web sites did undercut the best *Life & Pensions* quote, though others were quite a bit higher. However, overall the Internet quotes were below the *Life & Pensions* average.

## Insurance companies letting you apply online for their products

| Name of provider/intermediary | Web site | Main types of insurance available online | | | | | | | | | |
|---|---|---|---|---|---|---|---|---|---|---|---|
| | | Car | Home (buildings and/or contents) | Travel | Pet | Life (term) insurance | Critical illness | Traded endowment policies | Private medical insurance/ complementary medicine | Yacht and boat | Small business |
| Direct Line | www.directline.co.uk | ✓ | ✓ | ✓ | ✓ | ✓ | ✗ | ✗ | ✗ | ✗ | ✗ |
| Eagle Star Direct | www.eaglestardirect.co.uk | ✓ | ✓ | ✓ | ✗ | ✓ | ✗ | ✗ | ✗ | ✓ | ✗ |
| Elephant (part of Admiral) | www.elephant.co.uk | ✓ | ✓ | ✓ | ✗ | ✗ | ✗ | ✗ | ✓ | ✗ | ✗ |
| Halifax | www.halifax.co.uk | ✗ | ✓ | ✓ | ✗ | ✗ | ✗ | ✗ | ✗ | ✗ | ✗ |
| Hiscox | www.hiscoxonline.co.uk | ✗ | ✓¹ | ✓ | ✗ | ✓ | ✗ | ✗ | ✗ | ✗ | ✗ |
| Legal & General | www.landg.com | ✓ | ✓ | ²✓ | ✗ | ✓ | ✗ | ✗ | ✗ | ✗ | ✗ |
| Navigators & General | www.navigatorsandgeneral.com | ✗ | ✗ | ✗ | ✗ | ✗ | ✗ | ✗ | ✗ | ✓ | ✗ |
| Norwich Union CGU | www.norwichunion.co.uk | ✓ | ✓ | ✓ | ✗ | ✓ | ✗ | ✗ | ✗ | ✗ | ✗ |
| Prudential | www.prudential.co.uk | ✓ | ✓ | ²✓ | ✗ | ✗ | ✗ | ✗ | ✗ | ✗ | ✗ |
| Tesco | www.tesco.com/finance | ✓ | ✓ | ✗ | ✗ | ✓ | ✗ | ✗ | ✗ | ✗ | ✗ |

1. Also offers separate policies for holiday homes.
2. Travel insurance can be included as part of home insurance policy.

**Examples of life insurance quotes online and offline**

The table below shows the monthly premium quoted in July 2001 for a woman who is aged 45 next birthday and who is a non-smoker, taking out £100,000 of cover for 10 years.

| Web site | Cheapest quote | Insurance company providing cheapest quote |
| --- | --- | --- |
| www.egg.com | £14.25 | Prudential |
| www.ins-site.co.uk | £11.72 | Lutine |
| www.lifehug.co.uk | £12.07 | Friends Provident |
| www.moneyextra.co.uk | £9.30 | Legal & General |
| www.moneysupermarket.com | £9.75 | Lutine |
| uk.finance.yahoo.com | £11.50 | Legal & General |

**Equivalent quotes from *Moneyfacts Life & Pensions* magazine**

| Cheapest | £10.42 | Tesco |
| --- | --- | --- |
| Average | £17.08 | n/a |
| Highest | £48.60[1] | B&CE Insurance |

1. For workers in the construction industry.

Be aware that policies from the same insurance company may have different premiums depending on which web site you buy through. This reflects the different deals that have been struck with the provider regarding the commission paid to the web site and any other intermediaries involved. So shop around several sites.

Where the Internet does come into its own is in letting you arrange cover quickly and around the clock. If you've left it late to renew your car insurance, you can still shop around a bit and take out instant cover over the Net even if there is no time left to shop around by phone. Similarly, if you've booked a last-minute holiday, you don't need to take out the tour operator's expensive cover in desperation – you can instantly sort out a cheaper deal online.

The table on page 167 summarises a selection of broker and product-comparison sites according to the types of insurance

## Insurance brokers and product-comparison sites where you apply online for insurance products

| Name of provider/ intermediary | Web site | Main types of insurance available online | | | | | | | | | |
|---|---|---|---|---|---|---|---|---|---|---|---|
| | | Car | Home (buildings and/or contents) | Travel | Pet | Life (term) insurance | Critical illness | Traded endowment policies | Private medical insurance/ complementary medicine | Yacht and boat | Small business |
| AA | www.theaa.com | ✓ | ✓ | ✓ | ✗ | ✗ | ✗ | ✗ | ✗ | ✗ | ✗ |
| Easy Cover | www.easycover.com | ✓ | ✓ | ✓ | ✓ | ✗ | ✗ | ✗ | ✗ | ✗ | ✗ |
| Egg | www.egg.com | ✓ | ✓ | ✓ | ✗ | ✓ | ✓ | ✗ | ✗ | ✗ | ✗ |
| Interactive Investor | www.iii.co.uk | ✓[1] | ✓[2] | ✗ | ✗ | ✓[3] | ✓[3] | ✗ | ✗ | ✗ | ✗ |
| Inspop | www.inspop.com | ✓ | ✓ | ✓ | ✓ | ✗ | ✗ | ✗ | ✗ | ✗ | ✗ |
| Ins-site | www.ins-site.co.uk | ✗ | ✗ | ✗ | ✓ | ✓ | ✓ | ✗ | ✗ | ✓ | ✓ |
| Insurance Wide | www.insurancewide.com | ✓ | ✓ | ✓ | ✗ | ✓ | ✓ | ✗ | ✗ | ✗ | ✓ |
| Insure (web site of insurance broker Boncaster) | www.insure.co.uk | ✓ | ✓ | ✓ | ✗ | ✓ | ✓ | ✗ | ✗ | ✗ | ✗ |
| 1st4TEPs | www.1st4teps.co.uk | ✗ | ✗ | ✗ | ✗ | ✗ | ✗ | ✓ | ✗ | ✗ | ✗ |
| 1st Quote | www.1stquote.co.uk | ✓ | ✗ | ✓ | ✓ | ✗ | ✓ | ✓ | ✓ | ✓ | ✓ |
| Its4me | www.its4me.co.uk | ✓ | ✗[4] | ✗[4] | ✓ | ✗ | ✓ | ✗ | ✓ | ✗ | ✗ |
| Life Hug | www.lifehug.co.uk | ✗ | ✗ | ✓ | ✗ | ✓ | ✓ | ✗ | ✓ | ✗ | ✗ |
| MoneyeXtra | www.moneyextra.co.uk | ✗[4] | ✓ | ✓ | ✗ | ✓ | ✗ | ✗ | ✗ | ✗ | ✗ |

| Name of provider/ intermediary | Web site | Main types of insurance available online | | | | | | | | | |
|---|---|---|---|---|---|---|---|---|---|---|---|
| | | Car | Home (buildings and/or contents) | Travel | Pet | Life (term) insurance | Critical illness | Traded endowment policies | Private medical insurance/ complementary medicine | Yacht and boat | Small business |
| Money Supermarket | www.moneysupermarket.com | x | x | ✓ | x | ✓ | ✓ | x | x | x | x |
| The TEP Shop | www.thetepshop.com | x | x | x | x | x | x | ✓ | x | x | x |
| This is Money | www.thisismoney.com | x | x | ✓[5] | x | ✓[3] | ✓[3] | x | x | x | x |
| Yahoo | uk.finance.yahoo.com | ✓ | ✓ | ✓ | x | ✓[6] | ✓[6] | x | x | x | x |

1. Offered by the Its4me panel of insurers.
2. Provided by Hiscox Online.
3. Provided by Direct Life & Pensions Services (which also operates a site for intermediaries called Lifequote).
4. To be added to the site soon.
5. Provided by MoneySupermarket.
6. Provided by MoneyeXtra.

you can take out online. A name no longer on the list is Screentrade – one of the first and most successful online insurance intermediaries. Following its takeover by Misys International, Screentrade was closed down and, at the time of writing, it was not clear whether or not it would be reincarnated at some stage.

## Traded endowment policies

One specialist area of insurance that has recently entered the Internet arena is traded endowment policy sales and purchases.

An endowment policy is a type of investment-type life insurance. In the past, these policies have commonly been taken out as the savings vehicle to pay off a mortgage or as a stand-alone savings policy. However, as circumstances change, many people find themselves with endowment policies they no longer need – for example, perhaps they paid off their mortgage early with an inheritance and so are left with the associated endowment policy.

Endowment policies are designed to run for the long-term – policies usually have a lifetime of at least ten years and often as long as 25 years. If you cash them in early, you generally get a poor return (sometimes less than you had paid in premiums), because of the impact of surrender charges. Even if you keep the policy but stop paying the regular premiums (called making the policy 'paid up'), ongoing charges can eat heavily into the investment. But, provided yours is a 'with-profits endowment' (see the box on page 169), there is another option – you can sell your policy to someone else.

The price you get if you sell an unwanted endowment policy is usually significantly greater than the amount you'd get by cashing it in. You can also sell unwanted with-profits whole-of-life policies in this way. The new purchaser takes over paying the premiums and collects the payout at the end of the term (or on your death, if earlier).

To find out more, visit the web site of the Association of Policy Market Makers (APMM), the trade body for dealers in traded endowment policies (*www.moneyextra.com/apmm*). The site gives a brief explanation of the traded endowment policy market and lists the contact details of its members (with links to their web sites where they have them). The member firms can give you a quote if you have a policy to sell and can handle sales and purchases.

If you are in the market to sell an endowment policy, you can sell online through The TEP Shop (*www.thetepshop.co.uk*). Buyers can deal online through the associated site 1st4TEPs (*www.1st4teps.co.uk*).

---

## With-profits endowments

Investment-type life insurance, such as endowment policies and whole-life policies, works in one of two ways. Either your investment is 'unit-linked', meaning it grows directly in line with an underlying fund of investments, or it is invested on a 'with-profits' basis.

A with-profits policy grows as bonuses are added, usually once a year plus a 'terminal bonus' when the policy comes to an end. Once an annual bonus has been added, it can't be taken back. The amount of bonus depends partly on stock-market performance but also on other factors that affect the profitability of the insurer's business, for example, the costs it faces, claims made, dividends to any share-holders, and so on. The insurer also smoothes the bonuses by keeping back some profits from good years to add to bonuses in less good years. Therefore, a with-profits invest-ments should grow steadily.

Only with-profits policies, and not unit-linked policies, can be bought and sold on the traded endowment policy market.

---

# Borrowing online

# 11

The Internet can enhance the way you manage your borrowing by:

- helping you find the best loan or credit card
- letting you apply for a loan or credit card quickly and at any time
- giving you the convenience of being able to manage a loan or credit-card account online.

## Background information

For general guidance on borrowing, check out some of the personal finance sites, such as FT Your Money (*www.ftyourmoney.com*), Intelligent Investor (*www.iii.co.uk*) and MoneyeXtra (*www.moneyextra.co.uk*), which have a good array of guides, news and tools.

For advice on using credit wisely, visit the Office of Fair Trading (OFT) web site (*www.oft.gov.uk*).

If you do run into debt problems, don't ignore them – get some professional help fast, for example from:

- your local citizens' advice bureau (CAB) (see *www.nacab.org.uk* or *www.adviceguide.org.uk* to find your local branch)
- other money advice centres (try members of the Federation of Independent Advice Centres at *www.fiac.org.uk*)
- Credit Action (*www.creditaction.com*), a Christian-based organisation providing debt advice
- the Consumer Credit Counselling Service (*www.cccs.co.uk*).

# Finding the best personal loan

## How to compare loans

With a standard personal loan, you borrow a fixed sum for a set period of time and repay it by making fixed monthly payments. To compare one loan with another, you might look at the amount you must pay each month; this is sensible because you need to budget for the repayments. But the monthly cash flow does not take into account the timing of the payments and any extra charges, such as upfront arrangement fees. To weigh up cost more accurately, you need to compare each loan's annual percentage rate (APR).

It is not necessary to get to grips with how the APR is worked out; you just need to be aware that APRs show the cost of borrowing on a standardised basis, so you can directly compare the APR on one loan with the APR on another. The loan with the higher APR is more expensive.

Beware that neither the monthly cash flow nor the APR takes into account any charges that might be levied if you decide to pay off the loan earlier than originally planned, so you should check whether there is a redemption fee.

Most lenders offer you credit insurance (also called 'loan protection insurance') when you take out a loan. This takes over the monthly payments if you can't work because of illness or unemployment. You can choose whether or not to take out the insurance. If you do, the premiums are added to your monthly payments and reflected in the APR. When comparing one loan with another, make sure you compare like with like. If one loan includes insurance, you should compare it against the cost of other loans also including insurance.

This chapter focuses mainly on standard unsecured personal loans, but there are variations. For example, some lenders offer flexible loans, where you have an agreed maximum loan available to you that you draw on using a cheque book. You choose how much you want to repay each month subject to a minimum amount, such as one-twentieth or 3 per cent of the maximum loan.

Another option is to take out a 'secured loan' – this is a mortgage against your home. The loan is cheaper than an unsecured loan but, if you don't keep up the repayments, the lender can sell your home in order to recover its money.

## Internet-only deals

Many lenders (banks, building societies and financial companies) offer their loans through a variety of outlets – branch, post, phone and Internet. A few offer deals that are available only over the Internet. The table below shows the Internet-only deals that were available in July 2001 compared with other unsecured personal loans available at the time. The Internet-only group included some attractive deals, but not the cheapest, and, if you chose badly, an Internet-only deal could have cost a lot more than a loan from another lender. You need to shop around across the whole range of lenders – don't just assume the Internet is best.

### Internet-only *vs.* other unsecured personal loans

| Lender | Web site | Cost of £5,000 borrowed for three years (no credit insurance) | |
|---|---|---|---|
| | | **Monthly repayment** | **APR** |
| **Internet-only unsecured personal loans** | | | |
| AA | www.theaa.com | £160.11 | 9.9% |
| Abbey National | www.abbeynational.co.uk | £158.61 | 9.2% |
| Bank of Scotland | www.bankofscotland.co.uk | £160.11 | 9.9% |
| Goloan | www.goloan.co.uk | £164.50 | 11.9% |
| MBNA Europe | www.MBNA.com/europe | £167.82 | 13.5% |
| Paragon | www.paragon-finance.co.uk | £166.62 | 12.9% |
| Royal Bank of Scotland | www.rbos.co.uk | £169.30 | 13.8% |
| Smile | www.smile.co.uk | £164.05 | 11.4% |
| Tesco | www.tesco.com/finance | £158.30 | 9.1% |
| **Unsecured loans not just available by Internet** | | | |
| Cheapest | | £157.19 | 8.5% |
| Most expensive | | £180.82 | 19.5% |

*Source: Moneyfacts,* July 2001

## *Shopping around*

This is where the Internet really comes up trumps. Several of the product-comparison sites have excellent databases, updated daily, that you can search for the best loan for you.

Typically, you fill in a short questionnaire that asks some or all of the following:

- are you borrowing on your own or jointly?
- how much do you want to borrow?
- for how long?
- what is your date of birth?
- do you have an adverse credit record?

The search then comes up with a list of loans, generally ranked in order of increasing cost.

The table below summarises four of the product-comparison sites that we rated as particularly good. When tested to find the cheapest £5,000 loan over three years, all these services came up with the same result – the overall cheapest loan from the table opposite at 8.5 per cent APR.

### Web sites comparing personal loans

| Comparison service | FT Your Money | Money eXtra | Money Net | MoneySuper market |
|---|---|---|---|---|
| **Web site** | www.ftyour money.com | www.money extra.co.uk | www.money net.co.uk | www.moneysuper market.com |
| ***Number of personal loans/number of lenders on database*** | Over 400 loans | Over 55 lenders | Around 40 lenders | Over 400 loans |
| **Types of loan covered** | | | | |
| Unsecured personal loans | ✓ | ✓ | ✓ | ✓ |
| Secured personal loans | ✓ | ✓ | ✓ | ✓ |
| Car loans | ✕ | ✕ | ✓ | ✓ |
| Poor credit history | ✓ | ✕ | ✓ | ✓ |
| **Can you apply online?** | Some loans | Some loans | Some loans | Some loans |

## Applying for personal loans online

Many lenders – not just those offering Internet-only deals – now let you apply online for a personal loan. The quickest way to check out which online operators have a suitable deal is to use one of the product-comparison sites mentioned above. The results of a database search show which loans are available online. In many cases, the comparison site transfers you to the lender's own site to complete your application. Sometimes the application is handled at the comparison web site.

At present, you still need to complete the loan application by post as the contract requires your written signature. This is due to change, once regulations have been passed to allow electronic signatures.

## Handling your personal loan account online

In general, handling your loan account online is not standard practice. However, if you use an online bank, some – for example, Barclays (*www.ibank.barclays.co.uk*), First Direct (*www.firstdirect.com*), NatWest (*www.natwest.com*), Smile (*www.smile.co.uk*) and Woolwich (*www.woolwich.co.uk*) – let you include any personal loan in the accounts that you can call up online. And, at the time of writing, Cahoot (*www.cahoot.com*) was offering a flexible loan that could be managed completely online.

Combined accounts (see page 60) – such as Intelligent Finance (*www.if.com*) and Woolwich Open Plan (*www.woolwich.co.uk*) let you link your personal loan with current and savings accounts (and other borrowings), so that you pay interest only on the net balance.

## Finding the best credit card

There are a huge number of credit cards available, and which is best for you depends on how you use your card.

- if you tend to keep a balance outstanding on your card month after month, you should focus on the rate of interest (APR) you'll be charged

## Web sites comparing credit cards

| Comparison service | FT Your Money | MoneyeXtra | Moneyfacts | MoneyNet | MoneySupermarket |
|---|---|---|---|---|---|
| **Web site** | *www.ftyourmoney.com* | *www.moneyextra.co.uk* | *www.moneyfacts.co.uk* | *www.moneynet.co.uk* | *www.moneysupermarket.com* |
| **Number of cards/number of issuers on database** | Not disclosed | Not disclosed | Whole market | Around 40 issuers | Over 300 cards |
| **Types of card covered** | | | | | |
| Standard credit cards | ✓ | ✓ | ✓ | ✓ | ✓ |
| Gold and platinum cards | ✓ | ✓ | ✓ | ✓ | ✓ |
| Charge cards | ✗ | ✗ | ✓ | ✗ | ✓ |
| Donation cards | ✗ | ✗ | ✓ | ✗ | ✓ |
| Store cards | ✗ | ✗ | ✓ | ✗ | ✓ |
| Business card | ✗ | ✗ | ✗ | ✗ | ✓ |
| **Search/sort criteria you can use** | | | | | |
| Lowest standard interest rate | ✓ | ✓ | ✓ | ✓ | ✓ |
| Lowest introductory interest rate | ✓ | ✓ | ✓ | ✓ | ✓ |
| Interest-free period | ✗ | ✗ | ✗ | ✗ | ✓ |
| No annual fee | ✓ | ✓ | ✓ | ✓ | ✓ |
| Loyalty scheme/cashback | ✓ | ✓ | ✓ | ✓ | ✓ |
| **Compare what you could save against your current card?** | ✗ | ✓ | ✗ | ✗ | ✓ |
| **Can you apply online?** | Some cards | Some cards | No | Some cards | Some cards |

1. Search does not separate gold and platinum cards from standard credit cards.

- if you pay off your card in full each month, the rate of interest does not matter but you might be interested in a long interest-free period before payment is due, loyalty schemes or cashback schemes
- if you already have a card and want to transfer your outstanding balance to a new card, check out the introductory rate offered by the new card. But bear in mind that the introductory rate might apply only to the transferred balance, and your monthly payments would in that case usually be set off first against the transferred balance before any new purchases, so you might not get the benefit of the introductory rate for very long
- all cardholders should consider cards without any annual fee. Since there are so many competitive cards without an annual fee, you should only tolerate a fee if the card comes with some other feature that outweighs the detriment of the fee.

As with personal loans, the easiest way to check out credit-card deals is to use one of the product-comparison sites. The table opposite summarises five good sites.

## Applying for credit cards online

You can apply for quite a lot of credit cards online. All of the comparison sites in the table above, except Moneyfacts, note which cards produced by a search can be applied for online. In many cases, clicking on the link takes you to the card issuer's own site. In some cases, the application is handled by the product-comparison web site.

As with personal loans, you cannot, at present, complete your card application entirely online as you will need to sign the credit agreement. This should change when regulations are passed enabling digital signatures to be accepted.

## Managing your credit card online

Some credit cards – in particular Marbles (*www.getmarbles.co.uk*) and Egg (*www.egg.com*) – have been specifically designed to be managed completely online. But this does not mean they are the only cards offering the online option. Even seemingly staid and established providers, such as Barclaycard (*www.barclaycard.co.uk*), give the option of managing your account online. And, if you bank over the Internet, many of the online banks – for example, Bank of Scotland (*www.bankofscotland.co.uk*), Cahoot (*www.cahoot.com*), Co-operative (*www.co-operativebank.co.uk*), First Direct (*www.firstdirect.co.uk*), HSBC (*www.hsbc.co.uk*), Nationwide (*www.nationwide.co.uk*), NatWest (*www.natwest.co.uk*), Royal Bank of Scotland (*www.rbos.co.uk*) and Smile (*www.smile.co.uk*) – let you include credit cards in the accounts you can operate online.

Combined accounts (see page 60), such as Intelligent Finance (*www.if.com*) and Woolwich Open Plan (*www.woolwich.co.uk*), let you link your credit card with current and savings accounts (and other borrowings), so that you pay interest only on the net balance.

Managing your account online can be very convenient. With a traditional credit card, you touch base with your account just once a month when your statement arrives. In the meantime, you need to keep track of your spending to make sure you don't exceed your credit limit and you have no immediate warning if your card is being fraudulently misused. By contrast, with online access you can check your account at any time to see the balance or what transactions have been processed, and this also gives you the opportunity to spot if something is wrong.

With online access, you can pay your monthly bill online using a debit card, and may also be given other payment options, such as direct debit.

# Everything under one roof 12

If you've arrived at this page having read all the preceding chapters, you'll realise that managing all your finances online can result in a list of bookmarked sites as long as your arm and a head full of secret passwords and PINs. Wouldn't it be nice to have just one web site and one lot of security codes?

There are three types of service that aim to streamline managing your money online. The pros and cons of each are covered below.

## The one-stop shop

Some providers aim to meet all your financial needs from one web site, either with products from their own range or with products they have brought in from other providers. Typically, these sites offer banking and/or savings, investments, mortgages, insurance (and sometimes stockbroking too), all from a single site with access to all the accounts via a single identity code (ID) and single password. Prominent examples are Egg (*www.egg.com*), Virgin Direct (*www.online.virgin-direct.co.uk*), Halifax (*www.halifax-online.co.uk*) and Woolwich Open Plan (*www.woolwich.co.uk*).

Many online banks, while not offering a complete range of products, let you access current and savings accounts, credit cards, personal loans and mortgages through a single service. These include Bank of Scotland (*www.bankofscotland.co.uk*), HSBC (*www.hsbc.co.uk*), NatWest (*www.natwest.com*) and Royal Bank of Scotland (*www.rbos.co.uk*).

One-stop shops are obviously convenient. However, the drawback is that you are limited to the products of a single provider, or the narrow range they have chosen to offer, and you might be missing out on better deals elsewhere.

## One-stop bill paying

Convenience is also the motivation for a new service, Clear (*www.clear.co.uk*), which, when it is launched, will let you pay all your household bills online through a single web site. Clear aims to:

- alert you when bills fall due
- let you view and pay all your bills online
- give you access to your bills 24 hours a day, and
- act as an electronic filing cabinet keeping all your bill records together.

Services of this type go by the name 'electronic bill presentment and payment' (EBPP). Many gas, electricity, phone and credit-card providers accept payments via their own web sites, however companies such as Clear act as consolidation services allowing many bills to be dealt with from just one site.

EBPP services are widely used in the US, where the standard alternative is paper-based billing and payment. But they have yet to catch on in the UK. Here, the main beneficiaries of EBPP are the providers, who save the cost of posting out millions of paper bills.

The advantages for consumers are less obvious. The UK has a well-developed system for paying bills via direct debit, so you can already avoid the hassle of writing and posting cheques if you want to. And, if you are a lover of all things electronic, you may already have set up your Internet bank account to deal with bill payments (Chapter 5). However, a survey carried out for Clear suggests that more than half of UK households would like to pay bills online, and, of these, 80 per cent would prefer to use a consolidation service.

Whether consolidation services do take off in the UK remains to be seen. And they could be bypassed if account aggregation services (see overleaf) steal the show.

---

## Clear
## www.clear.co.uk

TYPE OF SERVICE: At the time of writing, Clear had yet to go live, but was planning to launch in late 2001. When it is operational, it will work as follows. You sign up with Clear and register the details of the companies that bill you. Clear lets all the companies know that you're a member. When a new bill arrives, Clear sends you an email alerting you that payment is due. You log on to the Clear web site and, over a secure link, view a summary and pay your bills by direct debit, debit card or credit card. If you want to see details of individual bills, you click on a link that takes you to the web site of the company that issued the bill.

CONTACT DETAILS: Follow the 'Contact us' link from the home page.

PRIVACY AND SECURITY: The policies are easily found on the site. Clear uses 128 bit SSL to encrypt information sent by and to you.

OTHER: Clear also intends to offer its service by WAP phone and interactive digital television.

---

## Account aggregation services

An account aggregation service is basically an intermediary between you and whatever online providers you have signed up with: for example Internet banks, online stockbrokers, investment fund services, and so on. The aggregation service gathers information (called 'scraping') from all the providers and brings it together in one place. When you log on to the aggregation service you are shown a summary of all your accounts. At present, to make any transactions, you usually have to go to the individual providers' sites (following a link from the aggregator's site, if you choose), but the intention is that eventually you will be able to run all your accounts from the aggregator's site. The main advantages of account aggregation are:

- convenience – you can view all your accounts on a single web site
- auto-login – in other words, automatic access to the account web sites. Using your stored security details, the service automatically links you to the various account providers without you having to key in each ID and password

- extra tools – for example charts to show how you hold your wealth, analysis of your financial arrangements from historical records, and so on.

The disadvantages are:

- concerns over security and privacy (see overleaf)
- the risks that either you'll forget the security details for the various accounts because you so seldom have to key them in, or, to avoid this, you write the security details down making them more vulnerable to misuse
- if you cancel your membership of the aggregation service, you would probably be wise to change all your passwords.

Account aggregation is another US import. The dominant service in the US is Yodlee (*www.yodlee.com*). Although not available in the UK, the Yodlee web site is worth a visit just to see how comprehensive account aggregation can be. Having logged on to the site, the user can access bank accounts, mortgage, credit cards, investments, bills, taxes, calendars, email, travel arrangements, news, e-shopping and more. Essentially it allows you to create a single, completely person-alised gateway to Internet services. At the time of writing, accounts from around 2,200 different providers could be aggregated on the Yodlee site.

In the UK, the only aggregation service currently available is Accountunity (*www.accountunity.co.uk*). By June 2001, the service had signed up 47 providers covering 120 accounts. But several other organisations are poised to offer aggregation services, including Virgin Money (*www.virginmoney.com*), which is already inviting people to register interest in its v-safe service, Egg (*www.egg.com*), Fidelity (*www.fidelity.co.uk*), Citibank (*www.citibank.com/co.uk*) and Barclays (*www.barclays.co.uk*).

## Security and privacy

Development of aggregation services in the UK has been hampered by concerns over security and privacy.

It is standard practice for online financial services, such as banks, to insist that you keep your passwords and other security data secret. If you don't, you are fully liable for any losses due to unauthorised use of your account using your ID and password (although as we have seen in earlier chapters, some services hold you liable even if you haven't disclosed your details). But for account aggregation to work, the aggregation service must have access to your security details so it can enter each account and gather information from it. This problem is being tackled in two ways.

With Accountunity, you do not disclose your security details to the service itself. Instead, the details are stored in encrypted form on your own computer. This means you have not disclosed the details to any third party. However, you should not treat information stored on your computer as secure unless you take proper security measures, including keeping the data behind a firewall and ensuring that you have installed up-to-date anti-virus software.

Alternatively, the aggregation service can negotiate with providers specifically to allow the passing of details to approved aggregation services. For example, the terms and conditions for Egg savings accounts state: 'If you want a third party to collect information about your Egg accounts from us, so that it can be aggregated with information about other accounts you have, you may be asked to give your security details and passwords to that third party. Before doing so, you must check that the third party is approved by us. We will not treat the disclosure of your security details and passwords to such a third party whom we have approved as a breach of you by the provisions of this condition.'

To make matters worse, the Financial Services Authority (FSA)* has made clear that account aggregation services do not fall within its sphere of regulation. This means there will be:

- no control over who can operate these services. However, if you go to a firm that is authorised by the FSA to carry on other activities, you should benefit from the rules requiring the firm to be solvent and run by fit and proper people
- no standard rules and regulations about how the services should be run

- no requirement for the service to have formal complaints procedures, should anything go wrong
- no access to an independent ombudsman if the service is not an FSA-authorised firm. At present it is unclear whether the Financial Ombudsman Service (FOS)* will be able to deal with complaints about aggregation services run by FSA-authorised firms
- no compensation if an aggregation service fails owing you money.

Aggregation services in the UK are for the time being also limited in the extent to which they can repackage the information gathered from the individual accounts, because the Data Protection Act does not allow alterations to be made to information from a third party's database.

However, the problems outlined above are likely to be overcome, and, if the US is anything to go by, in a few years' time account aggregation to handle your online finances may well have become the norm.

## Accountunity
## www.accountunity.co.uk

TYPE OF SERVICE: Summarises a wide variety of accounts that you hold with different providers (for example for your banking, savings, investment, share-dealing, and so on) on a single web page. Provides automatic links to each account without you having to key in each security code and password.

CONTACT DETAILS: Postal address easy to find through 'Contact us' from the home page. No phone number given.

PRIVACY: Policy easily found through link from the home page.

SECURITY AND LIABILITY: See the FAQ section of the web site. The security details of your individual accounts are encrypted using a very high standard, which is the norm. SSL generally used when sensitive information is transferred across the Internet. The encrypted details are stored on your own computer. How safe this is depends on the security measures you take with your own PC, however Accountunity suggests it is unlikely that anyone who did steal the data from your computer would be able to break the encryption. The details stored on your computer are not sent to Accountunity or any third party. When you log on, your computer talks direct to each account provider with Accountunity simply automating the process. You access the Accountunity service with an Accountunity ID and password. The terms and conditions warn that you use the Accountunity site at your own risk and that Accountunity will not be liable for 'any loss or damage whatsoever and howsoever arising as a result of your use or reliance on the information contained on the site'.

OTHER: Site contains a useful demonstration of how the service works.

# Financial advice online

# 13

The majority of financial Internet sites offer products on a no-advice basis. This is fine if you are happy doing your own research and making your own decisions, but it can be daunting if you are new to finance or feel you need professional guidance. If you fall into these latter groups, there are a couple of options open to you.

The first is to abandon the Internet route and seek out personal financial advice. The Internet can help you do this as there are now several sites that let you locate advisers in your area (see below).

The second option is to focus on the handful of web sites that are developing online financial advice (see page 189).

## Find an adviser

### Full financial planning and/or investment advice

As described in Chapter 2, any firm engaged in regulated activities, such as giving investment advice, must be authorised by the Financial Services Authority (FSA).* For many products – unit trusts, open-ended investment companies (OEICs), investment trust savings schemes, many individual savings accounts (ISAs), personal equity plans (PEPs), personal pensions and most investment-type life insurance – advisers must be either tied to a single product provider or independent and able to recommend any product on the market. If you want tied advice because you have already decided you are happy to buy from a particular company, you should contact that company, which will be able to put you in touch with one of its tied advisers. The rest of this section concentrates on finding an independent financial adviser (IFA).

There is no single trade body or organisation representing

## Web sites to help you find an IFA

| | IFA promotion | Society of Financial Analysts | Institute of Financial Planning | Association of Private Client Investment Managers and Stockbrokers | Ethical Investment Research Service |
|---|---|---|---|---|---|
| **Web site** | www.unbiased.co.uk | www.sofa.org | www.financialplanning.org.uk | www.apcims.co.uk | www.eiris.org |
| **IFAs covered** | Any type of IFA | Only IFAs with higher qualifications | Advisers who are Certified Financial Planners – most are independent but some are tied | Stockbrokers that offer financial planning and management services and specialist investment managers | IFAs who are experienced in dealing with ethical funds |
| ***Ways in which you can search for an IFA*** | | | | | |
| By postcode | ✓ | ✓ | ✗ | ✗ | ✓ |
| By broad geographical area | ✗ | By town | ✓ | ✓ | ✗ |
| By name of firm | ✗ | ✓ | ✓ | ✓ | ✓ |
| By method of charging (ie fees, commission or both) | ✓ | ✓ | ✗ | ✗ | ✗ |
| By area of expertise | ✓ | ✓ | ✓ | ✓ | All can deal with ethical funds |
| Other | Male or female adviser | ✗ | ✗ | ✗ | ✗ |

| Areas of expertise you can search by | IFA promotion | Society of Financial Analysts | Institute of Financial Planning | Association of Private Client Investment Managers and Stockbrokers | Ethical Investment Research Service |
|---|---|---|---|---|---|
| Retirement/pensions | ✓ | ✓ | ✓ | ✓ | X |
| Life and health insurance | ✓ | ✓ | ✓ | X | X |
| Planning for elderly (eg long-term care, equity release) | ✓ | ✓ | ✓ | X | X |
| ISAs/unit trusts/OEICs | ✓ | ✓ | X | ✓ | X |
| Tax/trusts/estate planning | ✓ | ✓ | ✓ | X | X |
| Ethical investments | ✓ | X | X | X | ✓ |
| Mortgages | ✓ | ✓ | ✓ | X | X |
| Investment and savings | ✓ | ✓ | ✓ | X | X |
| Investment trusts | ✓ | X | X | X | X |
| Offshore investments | ✓ | ✓ | X | ✓ | X |
| Shares/stockbroking services | ✓ | X | X | ✓ | X |
| Divorce | X | ✓ | X | X | X |
| Small business planning | X | ✓ | X | X | X |
| Other | X | X | Employee benefits, education expenses | Type of dealing service derivatives, stock market | X |

all IFAs. As a result, there are several web sites you can visit to get a list of IFAs, and each may give you a different set of names drawn from its own particular membership. The table below gives a brief comparison of the main services, including the ways in which you can search each site's database to find an adviser. Note that the areas of expertise listed simply show the way you can search for an adviser using the particular web site. A cross in the column does not mean that the advisers covered do not offer that type of service, only that you cannot cite that service as a way of narrowing down your search.

Having found an adviser, check that he or she is authorised before you do business. You can do this by checking the FSA Register* (*www.thecentralregister.co.uk*).

For general guidance on how a financial adviser can help you and how to get the best from him or her, check out the guides, booklets and factsheets on the various sites listed in the table on pages 186–7, in particular *www.unbiased.co.uk*, *www.sofa.org* and *www.financialplanning.org.uk* The FSA also publishes a useful guide to financial advice available from *www.fsa.gov.uk/ consumer*

## General insurance

General insurance advisers may be tied to one company, a handful of companies or be truly independent. If you want to select a policy from the full range available, you should choose an independent adviser. All members of the British Insurance Brokers Association (BIBA) are independent, and you can search the BIBA web site (*www.biba.org.uk*) for a member convenient for you. You can search either by:

- the county you live in, or
- what you want to insure – the search facility lists over 430 different categories of policy.

General insurance is regulated by a non-statutory body, the General Insurance Standards Council (GISC),* to which most providers and advisers belong. You can check out the code of conduct and see whether the adviser you've selected subscribes to it by visiting the GISC web site (*www.gisc.co.uk*).

## *Mortgages*

Mortgage advisers can be tied to a single provider, a handful of providers or be independent and able to recommend products from the whole of the market. At the time of writing, we were not aware of any web sites allowing you to search for a mortgage adviser. However, a new trade body, the National Association of Mortgage Brokers and Advisers (NAMBA) was in the process of starting up. It was intending to launch in early 2002 and was planing to include a 'find a mortgage broker' service on its web site (*www.namba.org.uk*).

Mortgage advice is regulated on a non-statutory basis by the Mortgage Code Compliance Board (MCCB),* which administers the Mortgage Code. You can read the Code and check whether an adviser you have chosen subscribes to it by visiting the MCCB web site (*www.mortgagecode.org.uk*).

## Web sites offering financial advice online

There is a very fine line between financial advice and the tools found on many web sites that help you to sift through a vast array of products. We can offer no clear distinction. A search tool that narrows down the list of suitable products to those fitting the criteria you have specified probably falls short of advice but may be little different from the task performed for you by, say, a real-world insurance adviser or mortgage broker. However, when it comes to investments there is a greater expectation that advice, as opposed to a mere search tool, will probe your personal circumstances and make judgements on your behalf about the products that may be suitable. In other words, advice may help to refine and set your search parameters.

Some personal advisers have long used computer programs to analyse their clients' needs and recommend suitable products from a database. One of the pioneers of this approach to financial planning was American Express which, having successfully offered the service in the US, introduced it to the UK in the late 1980s. But it is a new phenomenon for automated advice to be offered online without an adviser present to interpret and explain the computer's results.

At the time of writing, only three such services were

available to UK investors, the most comprehensive of which is CharcolOnline. However, the FSA is reportedly in favour of such services – automated advice generates clear records of the information gathered, advice given and mechanisms used to generate the advice, which makes these services easy to monitor and regulate. Therefore, it seems likely that more advice services will spring up, especially to support fund supermarkets (see Chapter 7).

---

## CharcolOnline

### www.charcolonline.co.uk

TYPE OF SERVICE: CharcolOnline is part of Bradford & Bingley plc. The web site initially dealt with mortgages but has recently branched out into investments as well. Two levels of personal assessment are available. 'Financial health check' is free and available to all. A series of questions check out your financial needs and arrangements for protection, borrowing, saving and investing. The system then generates a list of financial priorities, suggesting actions and broad types of product you should consider. However, CharcolOnline points out that the health check does not constitute financial advice. 'Fund adviser' is free but you have to register to use the service. You are taken through a comprehensive factfind that examines your objectives, assesses your attitude towards risk, checks out your existing financial arrangements and possible changes in your circumstances, among other factors. The factfind takes about 20 minutes to complete and generates detailed ISA investment recommendations. The service is regulated by the FSA. You can go straight on to invest through CharcolOnline's ISA supermarket (see Chapter 7) provided you have already opened a savings account with CharcolOnline. At the time of writing, the account offered a competitive rate of interest. All ISA purchases are paid for using money from the savings account. Documents relating to the savings account and your ISAs are only sent by email or stored on the web site unless you specifically request a paper version.

CONTACT DETAILS: Click on 'Call me' for a freephone number and email that you can use to request an adviser to phone you back. The postal address is buried in the 'data protection statement' (see 'Privacy' below).

PRIVACY: A brief privacy statement is given in the 'About us' section, with more detail if you follow the link to the full data protection statement. The information you give in the factfind is kept for six years in accordance with regulatory requirements.

SECURITY AND LIABILITY: You access the online advice and buying service using an identification name and password. CharcolOnline recommends you change the password frequently. The terms and conditions state that CharcolOnline is entitled to treat all instructions received using your security details as genuine and that all electronic orders received from you will be treated as your instructions even if you can prove that they were made without your authority. The site uses 128 bit encryption (the same high level used by online banks and most other online financial service providers. However, CharcolOnline warns: 'you must accept that dealing on-line, like dealing off-line, can never be 100 per cent secure, and you will not hold us responsible for any breach of security unless we have been negligent or in wilful default'.

## mPower Europe (formerly Sort)

**www.mpowereurope.com**
**www.sort.co.uk**

TYPE OF SERVICE: mPower Europe is an independent financial adviser. Under its former name, Sort, it provided advice by phone and Internet for a set fee. It did not sell products. The fee varied according to the type of advice being sought. It gave advice about life insurance, pensions and investment products, such as unit trusts, investment trusts, investment bonds, ISAs and mortgages. At the time of writing, Sort's services had been temporarily suspended following its takeover by mPower Europe. mPower is a US-based organisation that specialises in providing online advice in conjunction with other financial institutions. It is likely that the Sort service will be considerably changed and expanded when it is relaunched.

## WiseUp
## www.wiseup.co.uk

TYPE OF SERVICE: WiseUp is run by an independent financial adviser, Bates Investment Services plc. It operates an ISA fund supermarket (see Chapter 7) and, to support this, offers an 'Auto Advice' service. You complete a mini-factfind by answering questions about the type of ISA you want, your investment goals, attitude towards risk, how long you can invest, whether you have an emergency fund, and so on. The service then generates specific investment recommendations. You can go on to buy the recommended funds through WiseUp's link to the FundsNetwork (see Chapter 7) using your debit card.

CONTACT DETAILS: Easy-to-find postal and phone details, as well as email.

PRIVACY: Not found.

SECURITY AND LIABILITY: See 'FundsNetwork' (Chapter 7).

# Tax online

# 14

Most people have to pay tax on their income. If you are an employee or retired, you may well pay through the pay-as-you-earn (PAYE) system, whereby tax is deducted from your income before you receive it. However, each year around nine million people in the UK are required to complete a self-assessment tax return. This is likely to apply to you if you are self-employed, have tax to pay on capital gains or income from property, or if you act as a trustee, receive income from abroad, or have other complications in your tax affairs.

The tax return arrives in April just after the end of the tax year to which it applies, and must be returned by the following 31 January together with any tax still due for that tax year. If you send back the return by 30 September, the Inland Revenue* will work out your tax bill for you; otherwise you must do the calculations yourself. The table overleaf shows the tax timetable for the 2000–1 and 2001–2 tax years.

The table includes the dates by which you must pay tax for the relevant year. On 31 January during the tax year and 31 July following the end of the tax year, you pay two equal 'payments on account', which are generally set at half the previous year's tax bill. These are an estimate of the amount of tax due, and there is a final payment or repayment to square the bill on 31 January following the end of the tax year. By this time you should have completed your return and you will therefore know exactly how much tax you will need to pay.

The deadlines in the table are important. If you miss them you may be charged penalties and interest as shown in the second table overleaf. Around a million people missed the 31 January 2001 deadline for sending in their 1999–2000 tax return, and a further 400,000 or so who had sent in their form nevertheless failed to pay the tax due on that date.

## Tax timetable

|  | Year for which tax is due | |
|---|---|---|
|  | 2000–1 | 2000–2 |
| First payment on account | 31 January 2001 | 31 January 2002 |
| Tax return arrives | April 2001 | April 2002 |
| Second payment on account | 31 July 2001 | 31 July 2002 |
| Deadline for sending in return if you want the Inland Revenue to work out your bill | September 2001 | September 2002 |
| Deadline for sending in your return if you calculate your own tax bill | 31 January 2002 | 31 January 2003 |
| Final payment | 31 January 2002 | 31 January 2003 |

## What happens if you miss a tax deadline?

| Deadline | What happens |
|---|---|
| You want the Inland Revenue to calculate your tax but you fail to send in your tax return by 30 September | Inland Revenue can still do the sums for you but cannot guarantee to let you know how much tax you must pay in time for the 31 January deadline (see below) |
| You miss a payment on account | Interest is charged on the unpaid tax |
| You fail to send in your tax return by 31 January | Automatic penalty of £100 or the amount of tax due if this is less |
| You still have not sent in your return by the following 31 July | Further automatic penalty of £100 or the amount of tax due if this is less. Alternatively, Inland Revenue can seek permission to levy a penalty of £60 a day |
| You do not make the final payment by 31 January | Interest is charged on the unpaid tax |
| The final payment is still outstanding on 28 February | Surcharge of 5 per cent of the unpaid tax (plus ongoing interest on unpaid tax) |
| Final payment still outstanding by following 31 July | Further surcharge of 5 per cent of the unpaid tax (plus ongoing interest on unpaid tax and unpaid surcharge) |

# How the Internet can help

Since April 2000 you have been able to file your tax return and/or pay tax using the Inland Revenue's Internet service for self-assessment (*www.inlandrevenue.gov.uk/e-tax*). For 1999–2000 tax returns only, the government offered a £10 tax reduction to anyone using the service to both file and pay electronically. Fewer than 40,000 took up the offer (although more had registered for the service but did not use it) – far short of the Inland Revenue's target of 200,000 users in the first year. Undaunted, the Inland Revenue intends to be capable of handling half of all tax returns by Internet by 2002, and 100 per cent by 2005, though e-filing will continue to be optional.

Using the Internet to send in your tax returns and/or pay your tax bill can help you avoid missing tax deadlines. The Internet service is available 24 hours a day, seven days a week, and tax returns and payments are accepted immediately. If you rely on post or other methods of payment, you must normally allow at least three days for the return or payment to arrive.

Filling in your tax return electronically also has the advantage that many common errors, such as leaving boxes blank or forgetting to insert the date, are intercepted and corrected before the form can be sent.

To file your return electronically, you need to use either the Inland Revenue's own online tax form or commercial software, such as TaxCalc from Which?* (see page 200). The big advantage of these is that the software works out your tax bill for you, and this can save you a lot of time and aggravation. Commercial software usually has other features too, such as in-depth explanations of how the tax system works and hints on how you can save tax, but there is usually a charge of around £25 or so. However, this is inexpensive compared with using an accountant or tax adviser to sort out your return.

It is also worth bearing in mind that only 72 per cent of all self-assessment calculations were completely right first time in 1999–2000. This means errors were made in around 2.5 million cases. So, even if the Inland Revenue calculates your tax bill for you, you should still always check that the sums are correct. Using commercial software helps you to do this, and the tax saved as a result could easily outweigh the cost of the software.

The Inland Revenue online form is free but has a couple of drawbacks:

- it covers only the basic eight-page tax return and employment and self-employment supplements. If you need other supplements such as those for capital gains, share schemes or land, you'll have to look to electronic software
- you can complete the online form only while you are online, which (depending on the arrangement with your internet service provider – ISP) means you are running up phone charges. However, you can save a partly completed form and come back to it later, which is useful if, say, you need to go and find some paperwork. By contrast, you use commercial software offline until you are ready to submit your return.

Note that whatever software you have, you cannot use the self-assessment Internet service for sending in trust returns or partnership returns.

When it comes to paying tax, electronic transfers are more secure than sending money through the post. But you don't need the Internet for this – you can make an electronic transfer by giro at a bank branch or post office, or by using your debit card over the phone. And there are more ways to pay if you don't use the Internet: cheque or cash, as well as debit card or direct transfer. (The Inland Revenue does not accept payment by credit card.)

## How the Inland Revenue's Internet service works

You can browse the Inland Revenue web site, which contains comprehensive information about its Internet service and other areas of taxation, and you can even fill in the online tax return and print it out to post. However, if you want to use e-filing, first you must register. To do this, you will need:

- **your tax reference number** (a ten-digit number from the front of your tax return)

- **your postcode**
- **your National Insurance number** (on most documents you receive from your tax office).

You are also asked to give an email address (which will be used
to confirm your registration if it is successful) and to choose a
password. Your identification code (ID) is then posted to you
within the next seven days. Once you have it, you are ready to
access the online tax return. If you decide to use commercial
software, it will produce a tax return that you can then send
electronically using your ID and password. If you registered
last year, you do not need a new ID and password.

You need to be using Microsoft Internet Explorer version 4.0
or above, or Netscape Navigator version 4.72 or above. The
service is also available to Macintosh users.

To pay tax online, you need to register with a GiroPay
service called BillPay. A link from the Inland Revenue web site
takes you to the BillPay site, where you register by supplying
your name and address and choosing a password.

To make a payment, you key in your debit-card number, the
reference number from your statement of account, and details
of the amount you want to pay. The service is available
around the clock, seven days a week. Payments from £1 to
£19,999 are accepted. Provided your payment is accepted, the
Inland Revenue treats you as having paid tax on the date you
use the BillPay service. If the payment fails, it takes a couple of
days to notify you, so you could miss a tax deadline if you've
left paying until the last minute.

If you have an Internet bank account, you can set up
payments through your account (see Chapter 5) by entering
the Inland Revenue's bank details.

## Support

The Inland Revenue offers support by email and a local-rate
helpline. The helpline is available from 8am to 10pm Monday
to Friday, and 10am to 6pm on Saturdays and Sundays. You can
get help with all aspects of the Inland Revenue Internet service,
including its online tax return and BillPay. However, if you use
commercial tax software, queries relating to the software must
be addressed to the provider, not the Inland Revenue.

*Contact details*

In addition to the helpline above, you can also contact your tax office (the address is given on your tax return and other tax correspondence) or any tax enquiry centre.

*Privacy*

The Inland Revenue's Internet privacy policy can be accessed through the introduction to the service. The information you provide can be used for any Inland Revenue function, including tax, National Insurance, social security and tax credits, and some other purposes. The Revenue does not share information with third parties (except as required to by law).

To use the online tax forms service, your browser must be set to accept cookies.

*Security*

Currently you need an ID code and password to use the Internet service. You choose the password online, but the ID is sent to you in the post, and critics suggest this is a security weakness since your ID could be intercepted. However, the ID is firmly sealed in the same way as PINs sent by post, so you should be able to detect any tampering. Eventually, when they are more readily available, the Inland Revenue plans to switch to digital signatures, whereby you will be required to download a digital certificate, which is then used to verify that you are genuinely you.

Information passes between you and the Inland Revenue using a high level of encryption.

## Commercial tax software

The Inland Revenue site lists commercial software that has passed the Inland Revenue's tests for e-filing. The table on page 200 compares the software that was listed in June 2001, and includes web sites for more information and online purchases. Some software, including Which? TaxCalc, is also widely available through high-street shops and other outlets, or by phone from Which?.

## E-filing for businesses

If you run your own business and have employees, you can file your PAYE returns by Internet. As an incentive to do this, from April 2001 for one year only you qualify for a one-off discount of £50 if you file the return by Internet and also pay the tax due electronically. If you are also paying any of your employees' working families tax credit and/or disabled person's tax credit, you get a further £50 discount. You can find details of the Internet PAYE service on the Inland Revenue web site.

If you are registered for VAT, you can file your VAT returns and pay the tax by Internet. Again, as an incentive, for one year only running from April 2001, businesses with a turnover of less than £600,000 get a £50 discount if they pay and file by Internet. You get the discount when you file your first return of the year. For details see the Customs & Excise web site (*www.hmce.gov.uk*).

## Background information

The definitive web site for information about income tax, capital gains tax, inheritance tax and National Insurance is the Inland Revenue site (*www.inlandrevenue.gov.uk*). The site is packed with information, including all the leaflets and booklets that are also available from bricks-and-mortar tax offices. Navigation is reasonably clear and there is a search engine, so you should have no trouble finding your way around.

Another useful source is the TaxAid web site (*www.taxaid.org.uk*). TaxAid offers an advice service to taxpayers who cannot afford to go to an accountant or other mainstream tax adviser. In addition, it also keeps track of tax developments and campaigns for taxpayers' rights. Its web site contains information on how the tax system works, claiming tax credits, pursuing your rights, the latest tax news, and so on.

For VAT and excise duties, go to the Customs and Excise web site at *www.hmce.gov.uk*

## Commercial software for personal taxpayers

| Provider | Assured Credit Management | Consumers' Association | Digita | e-qua via |
|---|---|---|---|---|
| Web site | www.e-taxchecker.com | www.taxcalc.com[1] | www.taxcentral.co.uk | www.equavia.co.uk |
| Name of product | e-taxchecker.com | TaxCalc 2001 | TaxSaver 2001 Deluxe | Tax 2001 |
| Price (June 2001) | £19.99 + P&P | £22.99 to download or £24.99 incl. P&P | £29.99 + £2.99 P&P | £24.99 incl. P&P |
| **Tax forms covered** | | | | |
| SA100 Basic return | ✓ | ✓ | | |
| SA101 Employment | ✓ | ✓ | ✓ | ✓ |
| SA101M Employment – ministers of religion | ✓ | ✓ | ✗ | ✗ |
| SA101MP Employment – MPs | ✗ | ✗ | ✗ | ✗ |
| SA101MSP Employment – members of Scottish Parliament | ✗ | ✗ | ✗ | ✗ |
| SA101MLA Employment – members of Northern Ireland Assembly | ✗ | ✗ | ✗ | ✗ |
| SA101WAM Employment – members of National Assembly for Wales | ✗ | ✗ | ✗ | ✗ |

| Provider | Assured Credit Management | Consumers' Association | Digita | e-qua via |
|---|---|---|---|---|
| SA102 Shares schemes | ✓ | ✓ | ✓ | ✓ |
| SA103 Self-employment | ✓ | ✓ | ✓ | ✓ |
| SA103L Self-employment – Lloyd's | ✓ | ✗ | ✗ | ✗ |
| SA104 Partnership – short version | ✓ | ✓ | ✗ | ✓ |
| SA104F Partnership – full version | ✓ | ✓ | ✓ | ✓ |
| SA105 Land and property | ✓ | ✓ | ✓ | ✓ |
| SA106 Foreign | ✓ | ✓ | ✓ | ✓ |
| SA107 Trusts | ✓ | ✓ | ✓ | ✓ |
| SA108 Capital gains | ✓ | ✓ | ✓ | ✓ |
| SA109 Non-residence | ✓ | ✓ | ✓ | ✓ |

| Provider | Assured Credit Management | Consumers' Association | Digita | e-qua via |
|---|---|---|---|---|
| **Other features** | Tax payment schedule; lets you assess impact of, say, increasing pension contributions or changing a company car | Additional forms; selected Inland Revenue help-sheets and leaflets; comprehensive explanation of tax system; tax summary; tax-saving tips; extensive capital gains tax computations including indexation allowance and taper relief | Tax summary; tax calendar; online help including Inland Revenue helpsheets; tax-planning and tax-saving tips; tax calculators | Diary with key dates; online help |

1. In June 2001, security problems were discovered affecting users who had bought by credit card from the *www.taxcalc.com* web site. With advice from independent security experts, these problems were quickly rectified. We are confident that the site complies with the highest security standards and that you can safely shop online through *www.taxcalc.com*

# State pensions and benefits online

# 15

The government intends that all its services will be accessible via the Internet by 2005. So far, there is a wealth of government information available and you can print off many forms to complete and post, though interactive online government is still at an early stage.

## Finding a government service

All government online services can be accessed through UKOnline (*www.ukonline.gov.uk*). This is a portal designed specifically to help you identify the areas of government you need to contact, and it provides links direct to them. For example, the 'Life episodes' section lets you choose between going away, dealing with crime, having a baby, moving home, learning to drive, death and bereavement, looking after someone and looking for a job. If you click on, say, looking after someone, you are taken to a lengthy list covering every conceivable aspect of this life event, for example support centres, local social services, finding out about an illness, working out what help you need, financial support available, getting legal advice, balancing work and caring, and so on. Each topic links to the site of the relevant government department or other organisation that can provide the information, forms, and so on that you need.

The 'Quick find' section of UKOnline gives you access to an alphabetical list of all government departments, local government services and other bodies. Clicking on the name takes you to the web site of the department or organisation.

Other areas of UKOnline let you catch up with government news, download publications and respond to government consultations. A link to the 'Government gateway' enables you to sign up to interactive services, though at present the only such service available for individuals is the Inland Revenue self-assessment service (see Chapter 14).

An alternative (and older) site providing links to all government departments is *www.open.gov.uk* though this is less geared to the general public.

## Finding out about state pensions and benefits

State pensions and benefits used to be the responsibility of the Department of Social Security (DSS),* but from 8 June 2001 these have moved to the new Department for Work and Pensions* (*www.dwp.gov.uk*). However, at the time of writing, all the detailed information was still to be found on the DSS web site (*www.dss.gov.uk*). The departmental changeover has not affected the grass-roots agencies that deliver state pensions and benefits – for example, you still go to your local Benefits Agency for face-to-face meetings about benefits, and to the local Job Centre if you are seeking work. And, for some time to come, booklets and leaflets about state benefits and pensions are likely to continue to carry the DSS title and logo.

The DSS web site has three main sections for consumers: families and children, working age, and pensions and retirement. Clicking on any of these takes you to a list of topics leading to further information. For more detail, skip these main sections and go to the link headed 'Information for professionals and advisers'. Some of the information here is very technical but the so-called 'Technical guides' are very accessible to the lay reader. The table opposite lists some of the technical guides available in July 2001.

The professional and advisers section also includes many forms that you can download and complete to claim various benefits and pensions, and includes notes and details of where to send the forms. The table on page 206 lists the down-loadable forms available in July 2001.

If you want to talk to someone face-to-face about your state pension or benefits, you can visit your local Benefits Agency. Follow the link 'Your local office' from the home page for contact details of your local Agency.

## Technical guides to DSS pensions and benefits

| Number | Guide |
|--------|-------|
| DB1 | A guide to industrial injuries scheme benefits |
| HB5 | A guide to non-contributory benefits for disabled people |
| IS20 | A guide to income support |
| NI17A | A guide to maternity benefits |
| NP45 | A guide to widow's benefits[1] |
| NP46 | A guide to retirement pensions |
| RR2 | A guide to housing benefit and council tax benefit |
| SB16 | A guide to the social fund |
| WFL3 | Guide to personal adviser meetings and new deal for lone parents |

1. From April 2001, widow's benefits have been replaced for new claimants by bereavement benefits that are available to widowers as well as widows.

# Planning for retirement

In addition to the DSS web site, the government also runs an information site devoted to pensions (*www.pensionguide.gov.uk*). This includes guidance on stakeholder pensions and schemes run by employers, in addition to state pensions. The site is particularly useful if you are deciding what steps to take now to plan for an adequate income when you retire. The table on page 207 lists booklets that you can download from the site (or order as paper copies if you prefer).

### Retirement pension forecast

Although state retirement pensions on their own would not support a comfortable lifestyle, they do provide a core income on which you can build through your own additional savings. In deciding how much extra to save, it is helpful to have some idea of the amount you might eventually get from the state.

Some employers and personal pension providers are beginning to issue combined pension statements. These include details of your possible state pension alongside information about the private pension you are building up. However, if this doesn't apply to you, consider getting your own state retirement pension forecast from the DSS. You can do this by completing form BR19, available online. On the DSS

## Claim forms that can be downloaded from the DSS web site[1]

| Number | Benefit to which the form relates |
| --- | --- |
| (no number) | Back to work bonus |
| BB1 | Bereavement benefit |
| (no number) | Budgeting loans |
| CH2 | Child benefit |
| CMB1 | Child maintenance bonus |
| CSA1 | Child support maintenance – application |
| CSA1 | Child support maintenance – tax credits |
| CSA150 | Child support maintenance – earnings detail |
| CSA3 | Child support maintenance – maintenance enquiry |
| CSA3 | Child support maintenance – income support |
| CSA3 | Child support maintenance – tax credits |
| CSA6 | Child support maintenance – information from the mortgage lender |
| (no number) | Community care grants |
| NHB1 CTB | Council tax benefit |
| (no number) | Crisis loans |
| (no number) | Funeral payment |
| BG1 | Guardian's allowance |
| NHB1 HB | Housing benefit |
| SC1 | Incapacity benefit |
| IB1Y | Incapacity benefit – non-contributory |
| A1 | Income support |
| B16 | Income support – self-employed/sub-contractor[2] |
| DS7001/DS7002 | Invalid care allowance |
| MA1 | Maternity allowance |
| BR1 | Retirement pension |
| BF225 | Retirement pension – dependant's allowance[2] |
| SF100SM | Social Fund – sure start maternity grant |
| SF200 | Social fund – funeral payment |
| SF300 | Social fund – community care grant |
| SF401 | Social fund – crisis loan |
| SF500 | Social fund – budgeting loan |
| SSP1 | Statutory sick pay |
| (no number) | Winter fuel payments |

1. Available in July 2001.
2. Form can be completed onscreen or downloaded.

## Pension booklets available from
### *www.pensionguide.gov.uk*

| Number | Title |
| --- | --- |
| PM1 | A guide to your pension options |
| PM2 | State pensions – your guide |
| PM3 | Occupational pensions – your guide |
| PM4 | Personal pensions – your guide |
| PM5 | Pensions for the self-employed – your guide |
| PM6 | Pensions for women – your guide |
| PM7 | Contracted-out pensions – your guide |
| PM8 | Stakeholder pensions – your guide |
| (no number) | Women's info pack |

site, choose the main section headed 'Pensions & retirement'. Scroll down the list to 'Retirement Pensions Forecast [BR19]'. You can either print off the form to post or complete and submit it online. You'll need the following details to hand:

- your National Insurance number
- if you are divorced or widowed, the date of your marriage, spouse's date of birth and spouse's National Insurance number
- if you are divorced, the date of the divorce and your spouse's last known address
- if you receive child benefit, the dates of birth of your youngest and oldest children
- the type of National Insurance contributions you pay (if any)
- if you are or have been self-employed, the dates you started and (if applicable) ceased to be self-employed.

If you don't have all the above information, you can still send in the form, but it may take longer for your forecast to be prepared. In the usual way, the DSS asks you to allow 40 days for a response.

## Other sources of information

The UK benefit and pension systems are notoriously complex, and there are numerous advice agencies that publish information for consumers and can offer advice. A brief overview of some of these is given in the table overleaf.

## Other sources of information about state pensions and benefits

| Organisation | Web address | Benefit/pension issues on web site |
|---|---|---|
| Age Concern | www.ace.org.uk | Issues affecting older people. Downloadable factsheets deal with wide range of issues, including income-related benefits, housing benefit, council tax benefit, state pension, direct payments from social services, the social fund, attendance allowance, and so on |
| Child Poverty Action Group | www.cpag.org.uk | CPAG does not give advice direct to the public, but via its web site you can buy excellent guides to state benefits such as the *Welfare Benefits Handbook*, *Paying for Care Handbook*, *Child Support Handbook* and *Council Tax Handbook* |
| Citizens' Advice Bureaux | www.nacab.org.uk www.adviceguide.org.uk | Directory you can search for local CAB if you need face-to-face advice Online information about a wide range of issues, including benefits |
| Federation of Independent Advice Centres | www.fiac.org.uk | Searchable database to find a local money advice centre if you want face-to-face advice on issues such as benefit entitlement, managing debt problems, and so on |
| Help the Aged | www.helptheaged.org.uk | Issues affecting older people. Includes 'Information point' section with downloadable guidance on attendance allowance, benefits for carers, council tax, pensions, paying for residential care, widow's benefits and disability benefits |
| Local Law Centres | www.lawcentres.org.uk | Searchable database for your local law centre if you want face-to-face advice. Centres deal with legal issues including welfare rights, homelessness and, at some centres, disability rights |

| Organisation | Web address | Benefit/pension issues on web site |
|---|---|---|
| National Association for Managers of Student Services | www.namss.org.uk | Web site includes information about finance for students, including eligibility for jobseekers' allowance, individual learning accounts, and so on |
| National Council for One Parent Families | www.oneparentfamilies.org.uk | Helpdesk includes information on money matters, such as housing, maintenance and the Child Support Agency, students and money |
| One Parent Families Scotland | www.opfs.org.uk | Helpdesk includes information on money matters, such as back-to-work payments, bereavement, child benefit, the Child Support Agency, income support, maternity grants, and so on |
| Shelter | www.shelter.org.uk | Housing advice, including Shelter publications, such as the *Guide to Housing Benefit and Council Tax Benefit* |
| War Pensioners Agency | www.dss.gov.uk/wpa | Now part of the Ministry of Defence, gives comprehensive information about war pensions and how to claim them |

# Shopping online

# 16

A major factor holding back the growth of e-shopping is the fear that your credit-card details might be intercepted online and misused. As discussed in Chapter 2, this fear is almost certainly out of proportion to the reality of the risk. Provided you give your card details over a secure site (see page 23), the chance of them being captured by hackers is remote. However, if you are not convinced, there are alternative ways to pay for goods and services online.

## A second credit or debit card

A simple way to limit any risk is to use a second credit or debit card instead of your main one. Make sure a second credit card has only a low borrowing limit – say, £100 – and that will be the maximum that could be run up against the card if it were misused.

Similarly, you could open a second current account, one that includes a Solo or Electron debit card, and keep just a small balance in that account. With Solo and Electron debit cards, your account balance is checked before each transaction goes ahead, ensuring that you can't go overdrawn. Therefore, the amount you put into the account is the maximum that you could lose if your card details were misused. The main drawback is that, compared to credit cards, Solo and Electron cards are accepted on relatively few web sites.

In practice, it is unlikely that you would lose even the amounts described above. As outlined in Chapter 2, the Distance Selling Directive has been implemented in the UK; this means you are not held liable for any loss due to unauthorised use of your payment cards when buying most goods and services by phone, fax, mail order or Internet. The directive does not apply to financial products and services, but your loss with these is generally limited to a maximum of £50 up to the time you notify the card issuer that there is a problem, and nothing thereafter.

## Purse cards

Another option is to use a 'purse card' (also called a 'virtual purse'). This is a plastic card that you load up in advance with money. You then use the card to pay for things in online shops. The maximum you could possibly lose through misuse of the card is the amount you have loaded on to it.

Purse cards can also be useful if you are unable to have a credit card – for example you are under the age of 18 or have a poor credit record.

Prototype purse cards have been around for some years. For example, Mondex was a major experiment conducted in Swindon to test whether people would give up cash in favour of electronic money. When it comes to traditional methods of shopping it turns out that people are very much wedded to notes and coins for small purchases at least – but clearly this is not an option for Internet shopping, where purse cards have the potential to really come into their own.

Purse cards work rather like mobile phone pre-payment cards. You can apply for Splash Plastic cards via its web site (*www.splashplastic.com*) or from another source – for example some schools are distributing cards. The card comes with an activation code hidden under a tear-off strip on the leaflet accompanying the card. You need to go online to key in the activation code that brings your card to life, and to register a password that you should keep secret. Next you load cash on to the card at any authorised top-up agent; these include Carphone Warehouse outlets and 'Pay Point' and 'Pay Zone' terminals found in many supermarkets, convenience stores and so on. You hand over the cash at the counter, and the sales assistant swipes your card and keys in the amount. You are given a receipt, and once you return to your computer you should find that your card is loaded up with the cash and ready for a spending spree. The web site includes a 'Shop

Finder' to help you to find your nearest top-up point. You can also top-up your card direct from your bank account by standing order.

UK Smart (*www.uksmart.co.uk*) offers a similar service. Your account is called a wallet and you top it up with 'smart creds' – a currency you can use to buy things online from participating web sites. You can top-up the wallet by buying top-up cards from selected post offices. The cards come only in denominations of £20. You scratch off the security panel on the card and key this into your computer to transfer the credits to your wallet. You can also buy credits by cheque or standing order. To access your account and spend from it, you need to key in your user-name and a PIN number, which you need to keep secret to ensure your account is secure.

The drawback with purse cards is that the number of places you can top them up and use them to make purchases may be limited – at least for the time being. For example, at the time of writing Splash Plastic could be used in only 36 online stores, though a further 15 were due to be added. In the US, several purse cards have been launched but have failed, so it remains to be seen whether the UK versions will gain enough momentum to survive.

A further drawback is that purse cards are generally suitable only for relatively small transactions. This is because if you wanted to buy an expensive item, you might need to take a large amount of cash to a Pay Point, and carrying large amounts of cash is best avoided as it is not secure.

---

## Options for children shopping online

Purse cards are ideal for kids who want to spend their pocket money online. Another option – provided you trust your child to be financially responsible – is to make him or her an authorised user of your credit card. Although young people under 18 years of age cannot have their own credit card, they can be included as a user of someone else's card provided the card issuer allows it and the cardholder has agreed.

## Virtual currency

Few people these days receive a traditional pay packet stuffed with notes. Instead, an electronic transfer is made from the employer's bank account direct to your own. Come payday, your salary simply appears in your bank account ready for use. Perhaps, then, it is not too hard to imagine that one day you might get paid at least in part with virtual currency that can be used to buy things in the electronic world.

At present, there is no mechanism to pay you in virtual currency, but virtual currencies of sorts do exist. The main example in the UK is Beenz. So far, Beenz are used only as a promotional incentive. Online shops that participate in the scheme buy Beenz and then give them to you free when you visit their web site. Sometimes you get Beenz just for visiting, sometimes you have to buy something. You can then use your Beenz to get a discount when you buy something from a participating online store. To register for the Beenz scheme, visit *www.beenz.com*

## Internet shields

A further way to protect yourself online is to rely on a single company that you trust to act as a buffer between you and the Internet. In March 2001, Securicor – famous for its armoured vans transporting cash – launched an Internet shield service called SafeDoor (*www.safedoor.co.uk*). This service aims to keep your credit- or debit-card details secure and also to protect your privacy – another major concern with would-be Web shoppers.

You register with SafeDoor by giving the service your personal details and credit- and/or debit-card information. When you buy something from a participating online shop, you are given the option to transfer to SafeDoor to complete your purchase. The SafeDoor service checks your card account and handles the payment. This means you do not run any risks by passing your details to the retailer, and save on the time and inconvenience of filling in the retailer's order form.

If you do not want to pass even your name and address to the shop, SafeDoor can also arrange delivery to your home using its existing fleet of Omega vans.

The basic service is free to consumers, but if you opt for Securicor delivery there may be an additional delivery charge (on top of whatever the online shop charges you), though this is generally no more than £3.75 per delivery.

As with purse cards, the drawback of the SafeDoor scheme is the limited number of participating web sites. At its launch, around 40 online shops had signed up, though Securicor was planning to expand this to 100 by the end of 2001.

To set up an account on the SafeDoor web site, you need to enter your personal and credit- and/or debit-card details and to set up a password and other security arrangements. You can register as many payment cards as you like with just one SafeDoor account, giving you a choice of payment methods when you make a purchase. If you want to be ultra-cautious, you can register a second credit card with only a low credit limit and/or a debit card linked to a bank account with a low balance (see page 210).

Provided you keep your password and security information safe, and have complied with your card issuer's rules, Securicor covers any loss not already covered by your card issuer in the event of fraudulent use of your card.

The SafeDoor service is supported by a customer service helpline (calls cost no more than 10p per minute) that handles any problems, such as cancelling an order, exchanging goods, complaints and so on.

## Other ways to buy

Online retailers are all too aware that consumers are fearful of using their credit cards over the Net. Retailers also face the problem that card companies may charge the retailer up to 4 per cent of the purchase price as a commission for handling the payment. This makes small transactions uneconomic for many Web-tailers. There are various ways in which these problems are being tackled. You may come across the following methods of payment:

- a monthly subscription paid to the web site provider, in lieu of payment each time you use the service. For example, this might be used to charge you for receiving

information from a news site or downloading tracks from
a music site
- a premium-rate phone call. You might be asked to redial
  into a web site using a premium-rate phone line. Part of
  the cost of the call goes to the web site provider
- a charge via your internet service provider (ISP) account.
  The charge for a service might be added to the monthly
  amount you pay to your ISP if you are using a subscription
  service.

## Comparison of the main ways of paying online

|  | Credit card | Debit card | Purse card | Shield service |
|---|---|---|---|---|
| Perceived to be reasonably safe[1] | ✗ | ✗ | ✓ | ✓ |
| Any loss can be limited to an amount you choose (which can be low) | ✓ | ✓ | ✓ | ✓ |
| Can be used with many retailers | ✓ | ✗ | ✗ | ✓ |
| Suitable for large purchases | ✓ | ✓ | ✗ | ✓ |
| Retailer does not need to know your name and address | ✗ | ✗ | ✗ | ✓ |

1. Even though consumers perceive the use of credit and debit cards online to be
unsafe, facts suggest that in reality the risks are no greater than when using these
cards over the phone or in a bricks-and-mortar shop.

# Appendix I

## Which? Web Trader

### About the Which? Web Trader scheme

Consumers' Association* has been carrying out consumer research and publishing magazines and books for more than 40 years. Consumers' Association is a not-for-profit organisation that fiercely guards its independent and impartial status. It is probably best known for its flagship title *Which?*. The organisation launched its Internet arm, Which? Online,* in 1996.

In all its activities, Consumers' Association tries to achieve the following objectives:

- empowering people to make informed consumer decisions
- serving and promoting the consumer interest.

To support these aims, in June 1999 Which? Online launched the Which? Web Trader* scheme. The aim was to encourage the development of a safe and secure online shopping environment for consumers.

The core of the scheme is a consumer-focused Code of Practice with which online traders who are members of the scheme must comply. The Code changes as new legislation or 'best practice' emerges. Compliance is ensured by 'mystery shopping' exercises, monitoring of complaints, and customer feedback mechanisms including the Which? Online Forums. There are now 1,609 traders in the scheme.

## The Which? Web Trader Code of Practice

A trader displaying the Which? Web Trader logo on its web site agrees to follow the guidelines set out below. However, this does not mean that Which? or any of its associate companies recommends the products the trader is offering, or the customer service it is providing, outside the areas covered in the Code. The Code of Practice below was current in June 2001.

## What the trader must do

### General

Traders must provide clear and adequate information about their products and services to enable consumers to make informed decisions.

### Web site

The trader's web site must include:

- **the Which? Web Trader logo** incorporating the government's TrustUK logo on its web site, prominently so that consumers cannot miss it as they enter the site. The logo need not appear on the home page
- **full contact details** including phone and fax numbers, postal and email addresses, and a contact for complaints
- **the price of goods or services** – prices must be easily found and clearly shown in £s. The actual price the consumer will be charged – without any hidden extras such as tax, packaging or delivery must also be displayed
- **clear ordering instructions**
- **a description of the available payment methods** when buying goods or services from the site
- **a customer services phone number, the times when the service is available and the costs of the calls** – any customer-service staff must be aware of the trader's obligations under the Code
- **mention of the right to cancel the contract** and details of how to exercise this right
- **details of any restrictions**, including how long the offer remains valid and any cooling-off periods
- **an invitation to Which? Online customers to post comments about their experience** of using the service on Which? Online Forum discussions (Consumers' Association will invite the trader to comment on the discussions)
- **the terms and conditions of the contract**, displayed clearly and plainly. These must be easily found on the site. The trader must state that the terms of the contract do not affect your

statutory rights
- **arrangements to obtain the consent of customers to receive marketing email** from the trader or from others.

## Advertising

The trader's advertising must meet the standards of the British Codes of Advertising and Sales Promotion. In particular, it must be legal, decent, honest and truthful. The trader must also comply with the rulings of the Advertising Standards Authority (ASA),* details of which are available at *www.asa.org.uk*

The trader should also clearly identify any other advertising on its site, for example advertising or material from other organisations.

Finally, the trader must take care not to create a demand for its goods and services that cannot be met.

## Returns and refunds

If the trader has a returns and refunds policy that gives you more rights than those you have under the law or the Which? Web Trader Code of Practice, you must be clearly informed of this, with easy-to-follow instructions.

## Guarantees

If the trader is providing a guarantee or warranty, the following must be made clear:

- what is covered
- for how long
- that the guarantee or warranty is in addition to your statutory rights.

## The sale

Before the contract, the trader must confirm the price the consumer will pay. After the contract, the trader must confirm the order by email or post, immediately after the order is placed. The confirmation must include:

- the trader's name
- an order or reference number
- the total price
- instructions on how to cancel the contract, including to whom

the cancellation notice may be sent and whether you must pay for the cost of returning the goods.

Unless the law permits otherwise, the trader must give you the right to cancel the contract within seven working days without reason. In the case of goods, the seven days start when the goods are received. In the case of services, the seven days start when the contract was made.

If you cancel, the trader must return your money within 30 days of the cancellation. You may have to pay the cost of returning goods.

## Delivery

The trader must deliver the goods within 30 days, unless you have agreed to a longer timescale. If the trader cannot deliver the goods within this time, it should inform you immediately and agree on another time for delivery. If another time cannot be agreed upon, it must offer you a refund.

## Receipts

The trader must provide you with a receipt.

## Mistakes, complaints and disputes

- **consumer law** The trader must meet its obligations under the consumer protection laws currently in force. You can find out more about these at the web sites of the Office of Fair Trading (OFT)* (*www.oft.gov.uk*) and the Department of Trade and Industry (DTI) (*www.dti.gov.uk*).The trader must be governed by UK law
- **faulty goods** If the goods turn out to be faulty or different from those you ordered, the trader must offer you a full refund. The trader must give the refund as soon as possible, and at the latest within 30 days of agreeing to give the refund
- **mistakes in bills, receipts or payments** The trader must correct any mistakes in bills, receipts or payments as soon as possible, and at the latest within 30 days of agreeing to do so
- **complaints** The trader must have an effective system for handling complaints. The complaints procedure must be available online, must be easy to use and confidential. The trader must acknowledge complaints within five working days, advise you how long it will take to resolve the complaint and keep you informed throughout the process
- **disputes** The trader must provide details about any dispute-resolution scheme it belongs to, including any Ombudsman scheme or regulator.

## *Privacy and security*

The trader must meet the conditions of the Data Protection Act (DPA) 1998.

The trader must have a privacy policy and implement it effectively. If the trader does not have a privacy policy, it can use the policy outlined below, making any changes it needs to suit its business. The privacy policy must include the following:

- the trader must provide the consumer with the option to withhold personal information which is not needed for the transaction
- the trader must not collect sensitive personal information (as defined in the Data Protection Act) without the explicit consent of the consumer – for example, health or ethnic origin
- the trader must allow the consumer easy access to his or her own personal information
- the trader must ensure that personal information is accurate and up to date
- the trader should only hold personal information for as long as it is needed for the purpose it was collected
- the trader must tell the consumer if it is going to transfer personal information outside the European Economic Area
- the trader must provide the name of the person responsible for privacy matters
- the trader must display a clear and prominent statement before or at the time the consumer provides personal information, stating what information is being collected, how it is collected, who is collecting the information, what the information is to be used for, and whether tracking technology (such as cookies) is being used
- the trader must guarantee not to send the consumer email without first obtaining his or her consent.

## *Security policy*

The trader must have an effective security policy that it reviews regularly. The security policy must include the following:

- the trader must ensure that its web site is secure so that consumers' personal information and transactions remain confidential and cannot be interfered with
- the trader must ensure that the content of its site cannot be interfered with
- any subcontractors or third parties involved in the transaction

must follow these principles and maintain a similar level of security
- the trader must take steps to protect the Which? Web Trader and TrustUK logos against misuse
- the trader must provide information about the type and level of security being used on the site
- the trader must identify a person responsible for the security of the site. This person must regularly review the security of the system, make sure that any changes to the system are made in a secure way, and that the trader follows the security guidelines of the system supplier.

## What the trader must not do

### Unsolicited commercial email

The trader must not send untargeted mass-marketing emails to people it has never previously had any contact with.

### Children

Any communications aimed at children must be appropriate to their age and must not exploit their credulity, lack of experience or sense of loyalty.

A trader must not accept an order from someone it knows or suspects to be a child without the consent of the child's parent or carer.

If the child is under 12 years old, the trader must not collect any personal information without the consent of the parent or carer. If the child is over 12, the trader should only collect information necessary for sending the child appropriate communications as long as the child understands what is involved.

The trader must not disclose information collected from children to anyone else without the consent of the parent or guardian.

The trader must not ask the child for personal information about other people, or entice the child to give personal information by offering them a reward or a prize.

## What Which? will do

### Legal advice

Subscribers to Which? Online who have problems after buying from a Web Trader will be entitled to free legal advice from Which? Legal Service, subject to its terms and conditions. The trader must co-operate with Which? Legal Service to solve the problem.

## Dispute-resolution service

If the trader is unable to resolve a dispute with a consumer, it must inform the consumer that he or she may go to Which? Web Trader to have his or her complaint resolved. We will check to see whether the trader has handled the complaint properly, and if appropriate, recommend a solution. Our decision will be binding on the trader but will not prevent the consumer going to court.

Our independent service is free and available online to all consumers, no matter where they live. It is easy to use and quick, with clear time limits. We will file quarterly reports on its performance to TrustUK. If the consumer does not think that a complaint has been handled in accordance with these principles, he or she may refer it to TrustUK.

## Monitoring

We will monitor the effectiveness of the Code through feedback, complaints, mystery shopping and other research. We will deliver a report to TrustUK concerning the compliance of the traders on the scheme.

## Enforcement

If we discover that a trader has not complied with the Code, we will take enforcement action. We will investigate and, if appropriate, ask the trader to take action to resolve the problem. The trader must agree to take this action. If the breach is serious, the trader could be excluded from the scheme. There is an appeal procedure for the trader and we can provide details on request.

## Review

The trader must be informed of major changes to the Code of Practice, and will be given the opportunity to update his or her site accordingly. Help is available for traders with queries.

# Appendix II

## Web sites at a glance

### Chapter 2: Is it safe?

www.cookiecentral.com
www.fsa.gov.uk/consumer
www.thecentralregister.co.uk
www.which.net/webtrader

### *Which? Web Trader members – financial and property*

www.accountz.com
www.asdaforpets.com
www.abgltd.co.uk
www.azizcorp.com
www.boatinsure.co.uk
www.buy-insurance-on-line.com
www.checkmyfile.com
www.cipfa.org.uk/publications
www.directline.com
www.divorce-online.co.uk
www.elitemortgages.co.uk
www.etax.co.uk
www.firebrand.co.uk
www.flat-sharer.com
www.froglet.com
www.gfm-ifa.co.uk
www.insure4cover.com
www.insuranceshopperonline.com
www.jacksoninsure.co.uk
www.lmn8.com
www.moneymate.co.uk
www.nipropertysales.com
www.nis.ndirect.co.uk

www.pickasupplier.com
www.policydirect.co.uk
www.rapidinsure.co.uk
www.saveonyourbills.co.uk
www.scotflit.com
www.scotwills.co.uk
www.studentwatchout.co.uk
www.travel-insurance4u.co.uk
www.uswitch.com
www.weddingplaninsurance.co.uk
www.willsathome.com
www.wisemoney.com
www.wisebuy.co.uk

## Chapter 3: The advantages of e-finance

www.moneysupermarket.com

## Chapter 4: Getting started

www.btopenworld.com
www.find.co.uk

### Search engines

www.altavista.com
www.askjeeves.com
www.directhit.com
www.excite.com
www.alltheweb.com
www.google.com
www.hotbot.lycos.com
www.looksmart.com
www.lycos.com
search.msn.com
search.netscape.com
www.northernlight.com
dmoz.org
www.yahoo.com

## Chapter 5: Banking online

### Current accounts

www.abbeynational.co.uk
www.alliance-leicester.co.uk

www.bankofscotland.co.uk
www.ibank.barclays.co.uk
www.cahoot.com
www.citibank.com/uk
www.co-operative.co.uk
www.firstdirect.com
www.first-e.co.uk
www.halifax-online.co.uk
www.hsbc.co.uk
www.if.com
www.lloydstsb.com
www.nationwide.co.uk
www.natwest.com
www.netmastergold.co.uk
www.rbos.co.uk
www.smile.co.uk
www.online.virgin-direct.co.uk
www.virginone.co.uk
www.woolwich.co.uk

## Background information

www.bba.org.uk

# Chapter 6: Savings online

## Savings accounts

www.abbeynational.co.uk
www.bankofscotland.co.uk
www.barclays.co.uk
www.bristolandwestonline.co.uk
www.bristol-west.co.uk
www.egg.com
www.firstdirect.com
www.first-e.co.uk
www.halifax-online.co.uk
www.nationalsavings.co.uk
www.nationwide.co.uk
www.natwest.com
www.newcastlenet.co.uk
www.netmastergold.co.uk
www.rbos.co.uk
www.smile.co.uk

## Comparing accounts/background information

uk.finance.yahoo.com
www.fsa.gov.uk/consumer
www.ftyourmoney.com
www.iii.co.uk
www.lineone.net
www.moneyextra.com
www.moneyfacts.co.uk
www.moneynet.co.uk
www.msn.co.uk
www.thisismoney.com
www.uk-invest.com
www.which.net

# Chapter 7: Investment funds online

## Unit trusts offering online dealing service

www.abbeynational.co.uk
www.aberdeen-asset.com
www.abetterway.co.uk
www.ArtemisOnline.co.uk
www.barclaysfunds.co.uk
www.britannicasset.com
www.chaseflemingam.co.uk
www.csamfunds.co.uk
www.edfd.com
www.equitable.co.uk
www.fidelity.co.uk
www.gartmore.com
www.govett.co.uk
www.investecfunds.co.uk
www.jupiteronline.co.uk
www.landg.com
www.leggmasoninvestors.com
www.mandg.co.uk
www.marksandspencer.com/financialservices
www.martincurrie.com
www.mlim.co.uk
www.norwich-union.co.uk
www.perpetual.co.uk
www.rsainvestments.com
www.sarasin.co.uk

www.schroders.co.uk
www.scottishamicable.co.uk
www.scottishfriendly.co.uk
www.scottishmutual.co.uk
www.scottishwidows.co.uk
www.singer.co.uk
www.teachers-group.co.uk
www.standardlifeinvestments.co.uk
www.stewartivory.co.uk
www.threadneedle.co.uk
www.virgin-direct.co.uk
www.wesleyan.co.uk
www.woolwich.co.uk

## Fund supermarkets

www.ample.co.uk
www.bestinvest.co.uk
www.charcolonline.co.uk
www.chasedevere.co.uk
www.cheapfunds.co.uk
www.e-cortal.com
www.egg.com
www.fidelity.co.uk
www.fundsdirect.co.uk
www.hargreaveslansdown.co.uk
www.iii.co.uk
www.inter-alliance.co.uk
www.tqonline.co.uk
www.virginmoney.com
www.wiseup.co.uk

## Pensions

www.10direct.com
www.annuity-bureau.co.uk
www.annuitydirect.co.uk
www.discountpensions.co.uk
www.eaglestardirect.co.uk
www.hlpensions.co.uk
www.landg.com
www.norwich-union.co.uk
www.prudential.co.uk
www.sippdeal.co.uk

*Background information/fund
information/performance data*

www.aitc.co.uk
www.bestinvest.co.uk
www.bvca.co.uk
www.funds-sp.com
www.iii.co.uk
www.ins-site.co.uk
www.moneyworld.co.uk
www.netisa.co.uk
www.splitsonline.co.uk
www.trustnet.co.uk

# Chapter 8: Shares online

*Brokers*

www.alliance-leicester.co.uk
www.barclays-stockbrokers.co.uk
www.schwab-worldwide.com/europe
www.comdirect.com
www.dljdirect.co.uk
www.e-cortal.com
www.egg.com
www.etrade.co.uk
www.fastrade.co.uk
www.sharexpress.co.uk
www.h-l.co.uk
www.hoodlessbrennan.co.uk
www.idealing.com
www.imiweb.co.uk
www.killik.co.uk
www.mybroker.co.uk
www.natweststockbrokers.co.uk
www.nothing-ventured.com
www.selftrade.co.uk
www.share.com
www.sharepeople.com
www.stockacademy.com
www.stocktrade.co.uk
www.tdwaterhouse.co.uk
www.virginmoney.co.uk
www.xest.com

## *Comparing brokers/background information*

www.advfn.com
www.analystinsite.co.uk
www.apcims.co.uk
www.bloomberg.co.uk
www.blueskyratings.com
www.breakingviews.com
www.citywire.co.uk
www.digital-look.co.uk
www.etrade.co.uk
www.fool.co.uk
www.ft.com
www.ftmarketwatch.com
www.ftyourmoney.com
www.getrealtime.com
www.gomez.com
www.hemscott.net
www.iii.co.uk
www.inlandrevenue.gov.uk
www.liffe.co.uk
www.londonstockexchange.com
www.marketeye.com
www.moneyguru.co.uk
www.moneysupermarket.com
www.multexinvestor.co.uk
www.newsnow.co.uk
www.news-review.co.uk
www.proquote.net
www.proshare.org.uk
www.redskyresearch.com
www.riskgrades.com
www.schwab-worldwide.com/europe
www.sharecast.com
www.sharepages.com
www.stockacademy.com
www.stockpoint.com
www.uk-invest.com
www.updata.co.uk

## *New issues*

www.iii.co.uk/newissues
www.londonstockexchange.com

www.eo.net
www.barclays-stockbrokers.co.uk
www.schwab-worldwide/europe
www.imiweb.co.uk
www.sharepeople.com
www.stockacademy.com
www.stocktrade.co.uk

### Daytrading

www.directaccesstrader.com

## Chapter 9: Mortgages online

### Background information

www.cml.org.uk
www.fsa.gov.uk
www.ftyourmoney.com
www.iii.co.uk
www.moneyextra.com
www.mortgagecode.co.uk

### Lenders offering special Internet deals

www.mhbs.co.uk
www.netmastergold.co.uk
www.remortgages.co.uk
www.westbrom.co.uk

### Comparing mortgages/applying online

www.charcolonline.co.uk
www.creditweb.co.uk
www.fredfinds.com
www.ftyourmoney.com
www.iii.co.uk
www.moneyextra.com
www.moneyfacts.co.uk
www.moneynet.co.uk
www.moneysupermarket.com
www.ukmortgagesonline.co.uk

### Mortgage auctions

www.moneysupermarket.com

# Chapter 10: Insurance online

## Background information

www.find.co.uk/insurance
www.gisc.org.uk
www.insurance.org.uk/consumer2/consumer.htm
www.moneyextra.com/apmm

## Online insurers

www.directline.co.uk
www.eaglestardirect.co.uk
www.elephant.co.uk
www.halifax.co.uk
www.hiscoxonline.co.uk
www.landg.com
www.navigatorsandgeneral.com
www.norwichunion.co.uk
www.prudential.co.uk
www.tesco.com/finance

## Comparing insurers

uk.finance.yahoo.com
www.1st4teps.co.uk
www.1stquote.co.uk
www.easycover.com
www.egg.com
www.iii.co.uk
www.inspop.com
www.ins-site.co.uk
www.insurancewide.com
www.insure.co.uk
www.its4me.co.uk
www.lifehug.co.uk
www.moneyextra.co.uk
www.moneysupermarket.com
www.theaa.com
www.thetepshop.com
www.thisismoney.com

# Chapter 11: Borrowing online

## Background information

www.ftyourmoney.com

www.iii.co.uk
www.moneyextra.co.uk
www.oft.gov.uk

## Debt advice

www.adviceguide.org.uk
www.cccs.co.uk
www.creditaction.com
www.fiac.org.uk
www.nacab.org.uk

## Internet-only personal loans

www.abbeynational.co.uk
www.bankofscotland.co.uk
www.goloan.co.uk
www.MBNA.com/europe
www.paragon-finance.co.uk
www.rbos.co.uk
www.smile.co.uk
www.tesco.com/finance
www.theaa.co.uk

## Comparing personal loans/applying online

www.ftyourmoney.com
www.moneyextra.co.uk
www.moneynet.co.uk
www.moneysupermarket.com

## Comparing credit cards/applying online

www.ftyourmoney.com
www.moneyextra.co.uk
www.moneyfacts.co.uk
www.moneynet.co.uk
www.moneysupermarket.com

# Chapter 12: Everything under one roof

## One-stop shops

www.egg.com
www.halifax-online.co.uk

www.online.virgin-direct.co.uk
www.woolwich.co.uk

## One-stop bill paying

www.clear.co.uk

## Account aggregation services

www.accountunity.co.uk
www.barclays.co.uk
www.citibank.com/co.uk
www.egg.com
www.fidelity.co.uk
www.virginmoney.com
www.yodlee.com

# Chapter 13: Financial advice online

## Checking authorisation

www.thecentralregister.co.uk

## Background information

www.financialplanning.org.uk
www.fsa.gov.uk
www.gisc.co.uk
www.mortgagecode.co.uk
www.sofa.org
www.unbiased.co.uk

## Finding an adviser

www.apcims.co.uk
www.biba.org.uk
www.eiris.org
www.financialplanning.org.uk
www.namba.org.uk
www.sofa.org
www.unbiased.co.uk

## Online advice

www.charcolonline.co.uk
www.mpowereurope.com (formerly www.sort.co.uk)
www.wiseup.co.uk

## Chapter 14: Tax online

### *Background information*

www.hmce.gov.uk
www.inlandrevenue.gov.uk
www.taxaid.org.uk

### *Filing returns/paying tax online*

www.hmce.gov.uk
www.inlandrevenue.gov.uk/e-tax

### *Tax calculation software*

www.equavia.co.uk
www.e-taxchecker.com
www.taxcalc.com
www.taxcentral.co.uk

## Chapter 15: State pensions and benefits online

www.ace.org.uk
www.adviceguide.org.uk
www.cpag.org.uk
www.dss.gov.uk/wpa
www.dwp.gov.uk (formerly www.dss.gov.uk)
www.fiac.org.uk
www.helptheaged.org.uk
www.lawcentres.org.uk
www.nacab.org.uk
www.namss.org.uk
www.oneparentfamilies.org.uk
www.opfs.org.uk
www.pensionguide.gov.uk
www.shelter.org.uk
www.ukonline.gov.uk

## Chapter 16: Shopping online

www.beenz.com
www.safedoor.co.uk
www.splashplastic.com
www.uksmart.co.uk

# Glossary

**account aggregation service** Internet service that enables accounts held with different providers to be shown on a single screen and accessed by keying in just one set of security codes

**actively managed fund** Investment fund where the manager buys and sells investments based on his or her judgments about expected return, with the aim of producing superior investment performance.

**ADSL (Asymmetric Digital Subscriber Line)** Type of Internet connection that is much faster than connection via a modem over a normal telephone line

**AER (annual equivalent rate)** The rate of interest paid on a savings account or charged on an overdraft expressed in a standardised way that takes into account not only the amount of interest paid but also when and how often it is paid.

**annual percentage rate** The rate of interest and various other charges you must pay for a loan, credit card or other borrowing expressed in a standardised way that takes into account not only the amount you pay but also when and how often you pay. APRs can be compared to weigh up the relative cost of different loans and other types of borrowing

**anti-virus software** A special computer program designed to intercept viruses (destructive programs) on your PC and stop them from causing harm, or to fix damage caused by such viruses

**appointed representative** An adviser or salesperson promoting or selling the financial products of a particular company

**APR** Annual percentage rate

**arbitration scheme** A scheme for resolving disputes, for example between a provider and a customer. Arbitration is generally faster and cheaper than taking a complaint to court. The decisions of an arbitrator are binding on both parties to the dispute

**at best** Describes a deal carried out on your behalf by a stockbroker whereby the broker secures the highest available price if you are selling shares, or the lowest possible price if you are buying

**authorised** Describes a financial firm that is registered with the FSA and cleared to carry on certain types of financial business. In order to become authorised, a firm must be solvent, demonstrate that it is run by fit and proper people and in a sound manner. The firm must also agree to abide by rules, often governing the way it does business with its customers. Provided a firm you do business with is authorised, you have access to the Financial Ombudsman Service and Financial Services Compensation Scheme

**automated advice service** Computer program that generates financial recommendations based on the answers you give to a series of questions

**automated transfer** Electronic payment either into your bank account in accordance with instructions given by the person paying you, or from your account to someone else's account in accordance with instructions you have given to your bank. Payments can be by direct credit, direct debit or standing order

**BACS (Banks Automated Clearing System)** A system jointly owned by the largest banks for processing direct credits, direct debits and standing orders

**Banking Code** Voluntary code of business conduct observed by most banks and building societies

**basic-rate taxpayer** Individual who pays income tax at a top rate of 22 per cent in the 2001–2 tax year

**Benefits Agency** Organisation that through a network of local branches administers state pensions and benefits on behalf of the Department for Work and Pensions

**bid price** Price at which you can sell shares or unit trusts. It is lower than the offer price at which you can buy

**bid-offer spread** The difference between the bid price at which you can sell shares or unit trusts and the higher offer price at which you can buy. The spread provides income for the market-maker (in the case of shares) or the unit trust manager.

**bluetooth** An international standard being developed to enable electrical devices to communicate with each other using short-range wireless instead of being physically connected by wires

**Boolean operators** Standard symbols (derived from mathematics) that can be used with some search engines to make your searches more efficient

**branch-based account** A bank or building society account operated mainly from a physical (bricks-and-mortar) branch

**bricks and clicks** Describes a service available both from a bricks-and-mortar branch and also from an Internet site

**browser** Computer program used for navigating the Web. The two most common browsers are Microsoft Internet Explorer and Netscape Navigator

**bulletin board** Part of a web site where users can leave messages that can be read by all other users of that part of the site

**capital gains tax** Tax on the increase in value of something during the period you have owned it

**cardholder-not-present transaction** A debit- or credit-card purchase made by phone, fax, post or Internet

**carpetbagger** A person who opens an account with a mutual society, such as a building society or some insurers, with the main purpose of sharing in windfall profits if the society converts to a company or is taken over

**CAT standard** Describes a product the features of which meet minimum standards relating to its cost or charges, access and terms. CAT-standard products are designed to be straightforward and good value. They are not necessarily the most suitable product for you, but provide a useful benchmark against which to judge other products

**chatroom** Part of a web site where users can send messages to and receive messages from other users who are currently online at the same site

**cleared balance** The amount of money in an account and available for immediate use. This contrasts with an uncleared balance where at least part of the money in the account has only recently been paid in and could be cancelled if, say, a payment in by cheque were stopped

**combined accounts** Arrangement whereby the balances of several accounts (for example current account, savings account, mortgage, loans and/or credit cards) are pooled and interest charged or received on the net balance

**combined pension statement** Statement from the operator of an employer's pension scheme or personal pension showing how much pension you might get at retirement from that arrangement and also how much you might get from the state pension scheme

**commission** Money received by an intermediary for carrying out a financial transaction on your behalf. This can be money paid to an adviser by, say, an insurance company or unit trust whose product you have bought with the adviser's help – in this case, you pay the commission indirectly through the charges you pay for the financial product. It can also be money you pay direct to the intermediary, as is the case when you buy or sell shares and pay commission to the broker who handles your transaction

**Consumer Credit Act 1974** The main piece of legislation governing most credit contracts covering, for example, personal loans, hire-purchase agreements and credit-card transactions. It gives consumers some important areas of protection, for example making credit-card issuers jointly liable with the provider for faulty products bought using your card

**cookie** Information stored on your hard disk by a web site. It may include your user name and your own preferences, so that next time you visit the site it is customised for you

**corporate bond** A loan you make to a company that can be bought and sold on a stock market. Typically, the holder receives interest and repayment of the original loan when the set redemption date is reached

**county court judgment** Often abbreviated to 'CCJ'. An order by a county court requiring you to repay money you owe in accordance with the pattern of payments decided by the court. The court order is made as a result of the person to whom you owe money successfully taking you to court because you have failed to pay the debt as previously arranged

**cover** In the context of split capital investment trusts, extent to which the final redemption value of a 'zero' could be met out of current value of the assets

**credit insurance** Also called 'loan protection insurance'. Insurance that pays the interest on a loan or credit card if you are unable to work because of illness or unemployment. Such policies often have many exclusions, so you should check carefully before taking out the insurance that it is suitable for your needs

**CSV format** Stands for 'comma separated values'. A computer file format commonly used to enable spreadsheets and databases to exchange information

**current account** A bank or building society account that is the core of your day-to-day money management, enabling you easily to receive funds from other people and transfer money to other people's accounts. Typically, it includes features such as a cheque book, debit card, direct debits and standing orders

**cybercafé** A café or restaurant that has Internet-ready computers available for customers' use, usually for a fee based on the time you spend online

**Data Protection Act 1998** The main piece of legislation protecting your rights concerning the use of information you have supplied about yourself

**daytrading** Buying and selling shares over a very short time-horizon in order to make a profit from what are usually relatively small price differences

**debit card** Plastic card that acts in the same way as a cheque by transferring funds from your bank account to the account of someone else from whom you have bought goods or services

**Department for Work and Pensions (DWP)** New government department created in June 2001 which has taken over the functions of the former Department of Social Security and some of the functions of the former Department for Education and Employment

**designated professional body (DPB)** The trade body of a profession, such as accountants, solicitors or actuaries, which has been given responsibility for regulating the financial business of its members where that business is incidental to their main business activities. If financial business is more than incidental, the member firms must instead seek authorisation from the FSA

**digital certificate** System of encryption installed on your PC that, when used to send information to other people and organisations verifies that you are who you purport to be. It has the same effect as a written signature in the real world

**digital signature** The proof of your identity provided by using a digital certificate.

**direct-access trading** Another name for daytrading

**direct debit** Instruction you give to your bank to allow another person to take money automatically from your account on a regular basis

**discount broker** An intermediary that helps you to purchase investments, such as unit trusts, OEICs and ISAs, but does not offer any advice on the merits of the deal and sells you the investments at a reduced price compared with buying direct from the provider or through an adviser

**Distance Selling Directive** European legislation requiring member states of the European Union to pass laws giving consumers certain protection when they buy by phone, fax, post or Internet

**easy access account** Bank or building society account from which you can withdraw money on demand. But, unlike instant access accounts where cash is in your hands at the point of withdrawal, you may have to wait a day or two for a cheque to be posted to you

**EEA (European Economic Area)** Comprises Austria, Belgium, Denmark, Finland, France, Germany, Greece, Iceland, Ireland, Italy, Liechtenstein, Luxembourg, Netherlands, Norway, Portugal, Spain and Sweden. All but Iceland, Liechtenstein and Norway are member states of the European Union

**EEA-authorised** Describes a firm whose UK financial business is regulated by a body in its home country instead of being regulated by the FSA. The protection for consumers will be broadly equivalent, but not identical, to that afforded by the FSA

**e-filing** Submitting a tax return across the Internet

**Electron card** A brand of debit card that is notable because your account is checked prior to every transaction. A transaction goes ahead only if you have sufficient funds in your account, so it should be impossible for you to become overdrawn

**electronic signature** Another name for a digital signature

**emergency fund** A pool of money that you can draw on quickly and without loss should you need money at short notice. Typically, you keep an emergency fund in an instant access account or easy access account at a bank or building society

**encryption** The process of converting information into an encoded form that can be read only by someone who has the appropriate key to decode it

**endowment mortgage** An interest-only mortgage that you plan to pay off using the lump-sum proceeds from an endowment policy designed to mature at the same time as the mortgage term comes to an end

**endowment policy** Type of investment-type life insurance. An endowment policy builds up a cash value over a set period of time and is designed to pay out either at the end of that period or on your death if earlier. You can usually cash in the policy early but surrender charges mean you will probably get a poor return and may even get back less than you have invested

**Enterprise Investment Scheme (EIS)** A way of investing in shares newly issued by new and growing trading companies that gives you significant tax advantages

**Exchange Traded Fund (ETF)** A company whose business is running an investment fund, usually designed to track a particular stockmarket index and whose shares are quoted on the stock exchange. The price of the shares closely reflects the underlying value of the investments in the fund

**execution-only** Describes a stockbroking service whereby the broker carries out your instructions to buy or sell shares but does not offer any advice on the merits of your proposed transactions or recommend any deals to you

**exempt** Describes a financial business that is not required to be authorised by the FSA. It includes, for example, appointed representatives who are instead regulated by the provider they represent

**FAQs (frequently asked questions)** A section commonly found on web sites giving a mixed bag of information in a question-and-answer format

**fill or kill** Type of limit order where the transaction is either carried out immediately on the next trading day or cancelled if it is not possible to fulfil the order immediately

**Financial Ombudsman Service (FOS)** Independent complaints body that can adjudicate a dispute between you and a financial firm if you have failed to reach agreement through the firm's own dispute-resolution procedures. The Ombudsman's decision is binding on you but not the firm

**Financial Services Authority (FSA)** The UK regulator responsible for policing many areas of financial business

**Financial Services Compensation Scheme** Scheme that may step in to refund at least part of your losses if you have lost money due to the fraud or negligence of a financial firm that has gone out of business

**firewall** An Internet security system that protects a particular PC or internal network of computers

**fund supermarket** A single web site that sells the investment funds of several providers. These funds usually take the form of unit trusts and OEICs held either direct or through ISAs. Typically, a fund supermarket sells the investment funds at a reduced price compared with buying direct from the provider or through an adviser

**gearing** The practice of borrowing money to invest. If the investment grows by more than the cost of borrowing, the effect of gearing is to magnify the return on the investment. If the investment grows by less than the cost of borrowing, gearing creates or magnifies losses. In this way, gearing increases both risk and potential returns

**general insurance** Describes most types of insurance which are not long-term and either cover a limited period or have to be renewed

241

each year – for example, car insurance, home insurance, travel insurance and some types of health insurance

**General Insurance Standards Council (GISC)** Body responsible for a voluntary system of regulation for the general insurance industry

**gilt** Also called a 'British government stock'. A loan to the government that can be bought and sold on the stock market. Typically, the holder receives interest and return of the loan when the stock reaches its redemption date. A few gilts ('irredeemables') have no redemption date

**higher-rate taxpayer** Person who pays income tax at a top rate of 40 per cent in the 2001–2 tax year

**hurdle rate** In the context of split capital investment trusts, the annual rate at which the fund's assets must grow in order to pay the full redemption value to holders of zeros.

**income multiple** In the context of mortgages, the maximum loan you can have expressed as your income, multiplied by a set figure (the multiple)

**income protection insurance** Insurance whose payout is triggered if you are unable to work because of a long-term illness or disability and that replaces part of the income you have lost

**income tax** Tax on money that you receive on a regular basis in the form of, for example, earnings from work, profit from self-employment, interest on savings, and dividends or distributions from investments

**independent financial adviser (IFA)** An adviser who can recommend and sell you financial products drawn from the whole range on the market

**Information Commissioner** The official responsible for ensuring that the Data Protection Acts are observed and enforced

**information padlock** Symbol the Information Commissioner is encouraging firms to use to highlight to consumers that the firm observes the terms of the Data Protection Acts

**initial charge** A charge that you pay at the time you first take up an investment. Often the charge includes an amount that will be passed on as commission to any adviser who has helped you to invest. If you did not use an adviser (for example, because you bought through a discount broker or fund supermarket), the product provider may retain the whole initial charge. Alternatively, some or all of it might be rebated to you

**instant access account** Bank or building society account that gives you immediate access to cash either at a branch or through a cash machine when you want some or all of your money back

**interactive digital television** System that links your television to the Internet via your aerial or satellite and your phone line or via cable

**interest-only mortgage** Mortgage whereby your monthly payments cover only the interest due on the loan. Usually, you simultaneously make regular payments to an investment, such as an ISA or endowment policy that you hope will pay out a lump sum that is sufficient to repay the mortgage loan at the end of its term

**investment club** Arrangement whereby from three up to 20 individual investors formally pool some money in order to jointly invest in shares and other investments

**investment trust** A company whose business is running an investment fund and whose shares are quoted on the stock exchange. The trust's shares may trade at either a discount or premium to the value of the investments in the fund

**ISA (individual savings account)** Tax-efficient wrapper that you can put around a wide variety of savings and investments. Income and gains from the savings and investments in the account are free of income tax and capital gains tax

**ISA mortgage** Type of interest-only mortgage whereby you pay into an ISA each year and hope the ISA investments will grow sufficiently to provide a lump sum to pay off the mortgage loan at the end of its term

**ISDN (Integrated Services Digital Network)** A way of linking to the Internet that is faster and more efficient than using a modem and ordinary phone line

**ISP (Internet service provider)** Service that acts as a middleman connecting your computer to a much larger and more powerful computer that forms part of the Internet and so gives you access to other web sites

**key features document** Document that providers of certain financial products, such as unit trusts, investment-type life insurance and personal pensions are required to produce, describing the most important features of the product – for example, how much you must invest, the risks involved, the tax treatment, charges, and so on

**life insurance** Financial product that pays out a lump sum or income if you die. There are two broad types of life insurance: protection-only policies pay out only on death; investment-type life insurance builds up a cash-in value that can be paid out even if you do not die

**limit order** Instruction you give to a stockbroker to buy shares for you at or below a price you specify, or to sell shares at or above the price you specify. If the order is placed when the market is closed (called 'out-of-hours'), the limit order may operate on a fill or kill basis. Alternatively, a limit order can continue to be valid for a specified period – for example, a whole trading day or longer

**loan protection insurance** Another name for credit insurance

**loan-to-value ratio** In the context of mortgages, the value of the loan you are seeking as a percentage of the value of the property you are buying

**maxi ISA** An ISA that allows you to invest up to £7,000 in stocks and shares (and similar investments such as unit trusts), and may also give you the option to invest up to £3,000 in cash (in deposits like bank and building society accounts) and up to £1,000 in investment-type life insurance

**mini ISA** An ISA which can be either:

- a cash ISA allowing you to invest up to £3,000 in deposits like banks and building society accounts, *or*

- a stocks-and-shares ISA allowing you to invest up to £3,000 in shares, bonds, unit trusts and similar investments, or

- an insurance ISA allowing you to invest up to £1,000 in investment-type life insurance

**modem** A device that translates the digital signals of a computer into the analogue signals that an ordinary phone line can transmit, and vice versa

**money-laundering regulations** Rules that require financial providers to check proof of your identity and address before offering you products, in order to limit the potential for criminals to convert money from crime into seemingly legally sourced funds

**mortgage auction** System whereby instead of you selecting from a range of mortgage products, mortgage providers bid for your custom based on information you supply about your circumstances and needs

**Mortgage Code** Voluntary code of business conduct observed by most mortgage lenders and advisers

**Mortgage Code Compliance Board (MCCB)** Body with responsibility for ensuring that lenders and advisers who have signed up to the Mortgage Code observe its terms

**multi-tied adviser** Adviser who is able to recommend and sell you the products of a handful of product providers with whom the adviser has a business agreement. This method of selling is particularly common with general insurance

**National Insurance** Tax on earnings from employment and profits from self-employment. Payment of some types of contributions entitles you to certain state benefits

**new issue** The first offering to the public of shares in a company that will subsequently be traded on a stock exchange

**no-load fund** An investment fund that has no initial charge. No-load funds are usually available only through some discount brokers and fund supermarkets

**non-taxpayer** Person whose taxable income is too low for them to pay any income tax at all

**notice account** Bank or building society account whereby you have to apply a set period in advance if you want to withdraw some or all of your money or else lose interest

**OEIC (open-ended investment company)** Company whose business is running an investment fund. You invest by buying shares in the company from the fund manager. The price of the shares directly reflects the value of the underlying investments in the fund. Unlike a unit trust, OEIC shares are sold at a single price (with no bid-offer spread). The spread is replaced by separately quoted charges

**offer price** Price at which you can buy, say, shares or unit trusts. This is higher than the bid price at which you can sell

**PAYE (Pay-As-You-Earn)** System whereby income tax is deducted from earnings or pensions before they are paid over to you

**PEP (personal equity plan)** Tax-efficient wrapper you can put around investments in shares, bonds, unit trusts and similar investments. Since 6 April 2000, you have no longer been able to take out new PEPs but you can retain any PEPs you already had on that date and you can transfer the investments from one PEP manager to another. Income and gains from investment in a PEP are currently free of income tax and capital gains tax

**personal pension** Tax-efficient scheme for saving for retirement. You get income tax relief on what you pay into a personal pension, your investment builds up free of capital gains tax and partially free of income tax, and you can take part of the proceeds as a tax-free lump sum. Your money is normally tied up until at least age 50. Usually, you have some choice about how your savings are invested – for example, a choice of different investment funds or, in the case of a SIPP, your own selection of shares, funds and other investments

**PIN (personal identification number)** A code, often four digits but sometimes more, that you use to access an account. To prevent anyone tampering with your account, it is essential that you keep your PIN secret

**principal** Financial firm responsible for regulating the activities of an appointed representative

**pump and dump** Practice of talking up the value of a share by spreading rumours and gossip through chatrooms and bulletin boards and then selling at a profit before the price falls back

**purse card** Plastic card linked to an account, quite separate from any bank or savings account, which you load up with money. You use the card to spend the money in the account and, in the event of fraud, the maximum you can lose is the amount in the account

**repayment mortgage** Also called a 'capital and interest loan'. Your monthly payments pay the interest and repay the amount you originally borrowed. Provided you make all the agreed payments, the loan is guaranteed to be fully repaid by the end of the mortgage term

**residual shares** Also called 'residual stocks'. Shares whose sale and purchase cannot be settled through Crest, an automated settlement system. Because of the extra time and cost involved in completing transactions in residual shares, some brokers will not trade in them

**retirement pension forecast** A statement of the amount of pension you might get from the state at retirement, based on your record of paying National Insurance contributions

**search engine** Programs that let you search the Internet to find information on the topics you specify

**secure connection** Means of transmitting information to and receiving information from a web site whereby the information is encrypted so that it cannot be understood by any third party. If you are using a secure connection, a symbol – usually a closed padlock – appears on your computer screen

**secured loan** A loan, such as a mortgage, whereby the lender can sell something you own – usually your home – in order to recover its money if you do not keep up the agreed payments

**self-assessment** System for paying tax whereby you are responsible for working out and declaring any tax you owe on income received and gains made

**SIPP (self-invested personal pension)** Personal pension that gives you the freedom to choose what investments to hold within the plan. SIPPs are usually offered by stockbrokers and, because of the relatively high charges, are generally suitable only if you have a six-figure sum invested

**smart card** Plastic payment card that has a microchip embedded within it. The chip is capable of carrying large amounts of information, including security details, and is more secure from fraud and counterfeiting than traditional cards that rely on information carried on a magnetic strip

**Solo card** Brand of debit card significant because your account is checked before every transaction. If there is not enough money in your account, the transaction does not go ahead, so it should be impossible for you to become overdrawn

**split-capital trust** Type of investment trust that offers more than one type of share. Typically, the trust has a limited lifetime. 'Income shares' receive all the dividends paid out during the life of the trust and, on termination, receive either a set sum or no capital repayment at all. 'Capital shares' get no income during the life of the trust, but receive a lump sum on termination that is a share of the value of the assets held by the trust

**spread** The difference between a bid price and offer price

**SSL (secure socket layer)** A system of encrypting information so that it cannot be understood if intercepted by a third party

**stakeholder pension** Either a personal pension or employer's pension scheme that meets certain conditions designed to ensure that the arrangement is flexible and good value. The conditions include charges being no more than 1 per cent a year of the value of your investment

**stamp duty** Tax traditionally charged on various 'instruments' (documents) evidencing deals. Even when paper certificates are no longer involved, stamp duty is charged on purchases of UK shares

**standing order** Instruction to your bank to pay a set amount at set intervals from your account to the account of someone else

**starting-rate taxpayer** Person who pays income tax at a top rate of 10 per cent in the 2001–2 tax year

**straight-through dealing** Trading through an online broker's web site whereby you deal directly with the market (as opposed to sending your order to a human broker who deals on your behalf)

**sweeper accounts** Arrangement whereby surplus funds in a current account are automatically transferred to a savings account

**TESSA (tax-efficient special savings account)** Type of bank or building society account in which the interest you earn is tax-free provided you leave your money invested for five years. Since 6 April

1999, you have no longer been able to open a new TESSA but you can keep any TESSA already started before then and, when it matures, you can transfer your capital to a special TESSA-only ISA

**tied adviser** An adviser who can recommend and sell you only the products of a particular provider

**tracker fund** Investment fund where shares are selected to mimic the movements in a chosen stockmarket index and are bought and sold relatively infrequently only to reflect changes in the index constituents.

**Traded Endowment Policy (TEP)** An endowment policy that has built up a cash value and that you put up for sale as an alternative to cashing it in

**unit trust** An investment fund that you invest in by buying units from the fund manager. Each unit represents a slice of the fund. If there are more buyers than sellers, new units are created. If there are more sellers than buyers, units are cancelled. In this way, the unit price directly reflects the value of the underlying investments in the fund. With most unit trusts, there are two unit prices – the higher offer price at which you buy, and the lower bid price at which you sell

**unsecured loan** A loan that is not linked to specific possessions that you own. If you fail to repay the loan as agreed, all the lender can do to get its money back is take you to court. The court will assess your ability to repay and may make a county court judgment requiring you to pay the lender a set amount each month. However, this may be a lot less than the payments required under the original loan agreement. Because unsecured loans are more risky for the lender, they are more expensive than secured loans

**venture capital trust (VCT)** Type of investment trust that invests in the newly issued shares of new and growing trading companies. You qualify for various tax reliefs when you invest in a VCT

**virus** Destructive program specifically designed to 'infect' and usually damage other computer programs. It can alter and delete data, send data via email to other computers and cause serious computer malfunctions

**zero** Type of capital share in a split-capital investment trust. Provided there are sufficient assets in the fund at redemption, zeros receive a fixed pay-out when the trust is wound up.

# Addresses

**Advertising Standards Authority (ASA)**
2 Torrington Place
London WC1E 7HW
Tel: 020-7580 5555
Fax: 020-7631 3051
Email: inquiries@asa.org.uk
Web site: www.asa.org.uk

**Consumers' Association (CA)**
*see Which?*

**Department for Work and Pensions (DWP)**
Tel: 020-7712 2171
Web site: www.dwp.gov.uk
*See phone book under 'Benefits Agency' for local branches*

**Department of Social Security (DSS)**
*Now incorporated into the Department for Work and Pensions*

**Financial Ombudsman Service (FOS)**
South Quay Plaza
183 Marsh Wall
London E14 9SR
Tel: (0845) 080 1800
Fax: 020-7964 1001
Web site: www.financial-ombudsman.org.uk

**Financial Services Authority (FSA)**
25 The North Colonnade
Canary Wharf
London E14 5HS
Consumer helpline:
(0845) 606 1234
Fax: 020-7676 9713
Email:
consumerhelp@fsa.gov.uk
Web site: www.fsa.gov.uk

**FSA Register**
Tel: (0845) 606 1234
Email:
consumerhelp@fsa.gov.uk
Web site:
www.thecentralregister.co.uk

**Financial Services Compensation Scheme (FSCS)**
7th Floor
Lloyds Chambers
Portsoken Street
London E1 8BN
Tel: 020-7892 7300
Fax: 020-7892 7301
Email: enquiries@fscs.org.uk
Web site: www.fscs.org.uk

### General Insurance Standards Council (GISC)
110 Cannon Street
London EC4N 6EU
General enquiries:
020-7648 7810
Complaints: (0845) 601 2857
Fax: 020-7648 7808
Email (general enquiries):
enquiries@gisc.co.uk
Email (complaints):
complaints@gisc.co.uk
Web site: www.gisc.co.uk

### Information Commissioner
*(formerly the Data Protection Commissioner)*
Data Protection Commissioner
Wycliffe House
Water Lane, Wilmslow
Cheshire SK9 5AF
Information line:
(01625) 545745
Fax: (01625) 524510
Email:
mail@dataprotection.gov.uk
Web site:
www.dataprotection.gov.uk

### Inland Revenue
Web site:
www.inlandrevenue.gov.uk
*See phone book under 'Inland Revenue' for local tax enquiry centre*

### Mortgage Code Compliance Board (MCCB)
University Court
Stafford ST18 0GN
Tel: (01785) 218200

Email:
enquiries@mortgagecode.org.uk
Web site:
www.mortgagecode.co.uk

### Office of Fair Trading (OFT)
Fleetbank House
2–6 Salisbury Square
London EC4Y 8JX
General enquiries:
(08457) 224499
Publication orderline:
(0870) 606 0321
Fax: 020-7211 8800
Email: enquiries@oft.gov.uk
Web site: www.oft.gov.uk

### TrustUK
5th Floor
Haymarket House
1 Oxendon Street
London SW1Y 4EE
Tel: 020-7766 4455
Email:
secretariat@trustuk.org.uk
Web site: www.trustuk.org.uk

### Which?
Castlemead
Gascoyne Way
Hertford X, SG14 1LH
Tel: (01992) 822800
Email: support@which.net
Web site: www.which.net

### Which? Books
2 Marylebone Road
London NW1 4DF
Tel: (0800) 252100
Email: books@which.net
Web site: www.which.net

***Which? Online***
Castlemead
Gascoyne Way
Hertford X, SG14 1YB
Tel: (08453) 010010
Fax: 020-7770 7485
Email: editor@which.net
Web site: www.which.net

***Which? Web Trader***
Castlemead
Gascoyne Way
Hertford X, SG14 1YB
Tel: (01992) 822888
Fax: 0207-770 7485 (mark
'Webtrader')
Email: webtrader@which.net
Web site:
www.whichwebtrader.co.uk

# Index